Using Microsoft Word 2013 for Academic Papers

Contents

Page Layout

Microsoft Word is a popular word-processing program. It is capable of doing many things, and because of that, it is complex, sometimes difficult to use — and sometimes it does things we did not ask it to do. However, after we learn how to control Word, it will make the process of preparing papers much easier. We will find that it can do things we want it to do – we just need to learn how to use it.

This tutorial is designed for a variety of users. For beginnings, some of what we say will be too complicated. For more experienced users, some of what we say will be too simplistic. So feel free to skip the parts you do not want. But if you think something is too complicated, you might want to skim it anyway, just so that you'll know that such things can be done, if you ever need them. Store it away for a later day.

Our focus in this document is for academic papers. Other users will probably find this information helpful, too, but our focus is on academic papers. Some of the default settings in Word are designed for business use, and academic papers require different settings. So we need to learn how to change the settings in Word.

Paper size

Academic papers (for U.S. schools) should have 1-inch margins all around, on 8½ x 11 inch paper. The default paper size is probably already correct, but you may need to change your margins. We will illustrate how to do it with images from Word 2013 for Windows. Your colors may be different.

1. In the upper left corner of your screen, click on the "tab" that says "Page Layout." We have circled it in the the the image below:

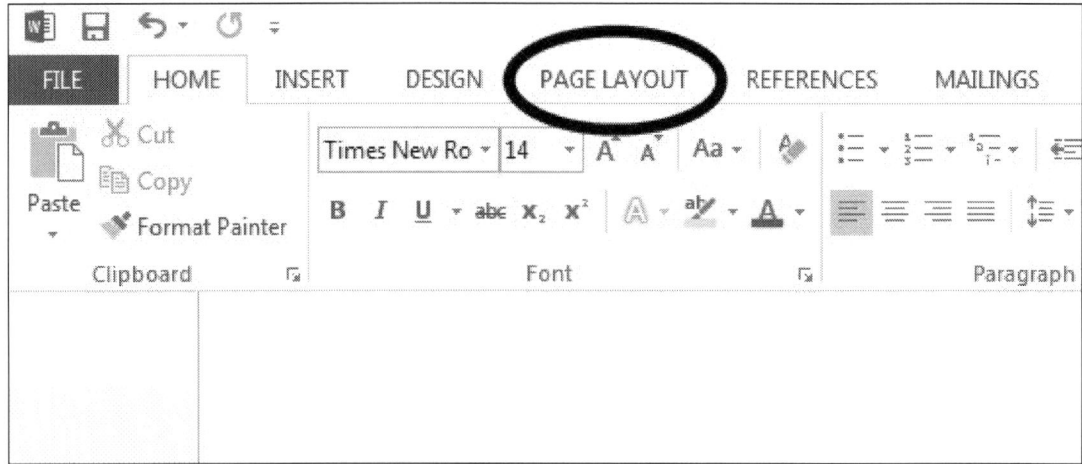

2. Then you will see a "ribbon" or strip of images ("icons") that can do different things for you. Here's part of what you'll see:

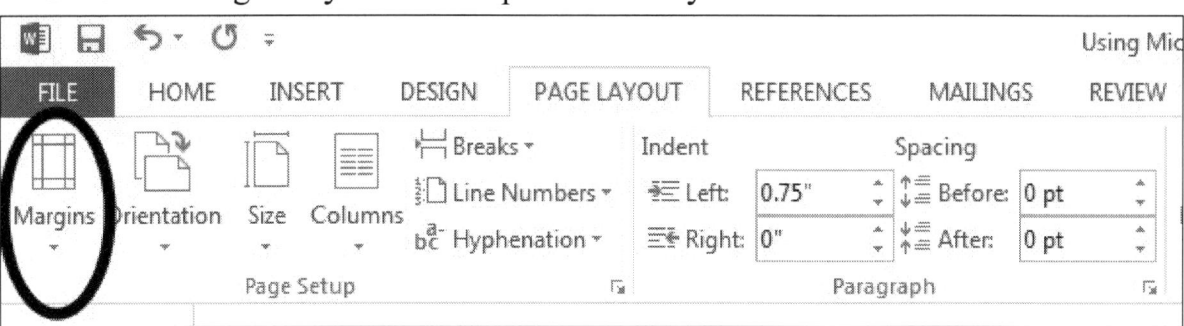

3. Click on the "Margins" icon, and a menu will drop down:

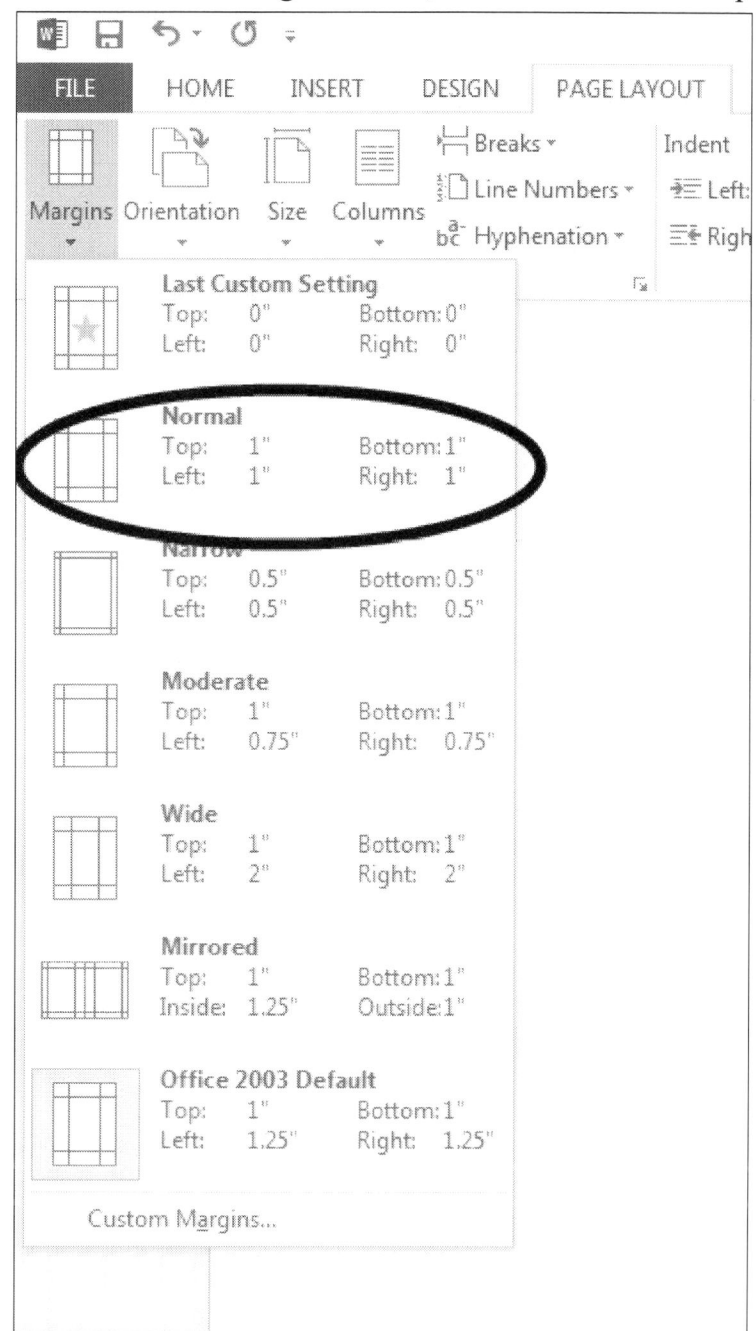

4. For an academic paper, click on "Normal." It is interesting that Microsoft thinks that 1-inch margins are normal, but they did not choose that as their default.

    After clicking on "normal," you are done – for this document. If you would like all of your documents in the future to have normal margins, then you need to change your default settings. To do this, instead of clicking on "Normal" in step 3, you need to go to the bottom of the drop-down menu and click on "Custom Margins."

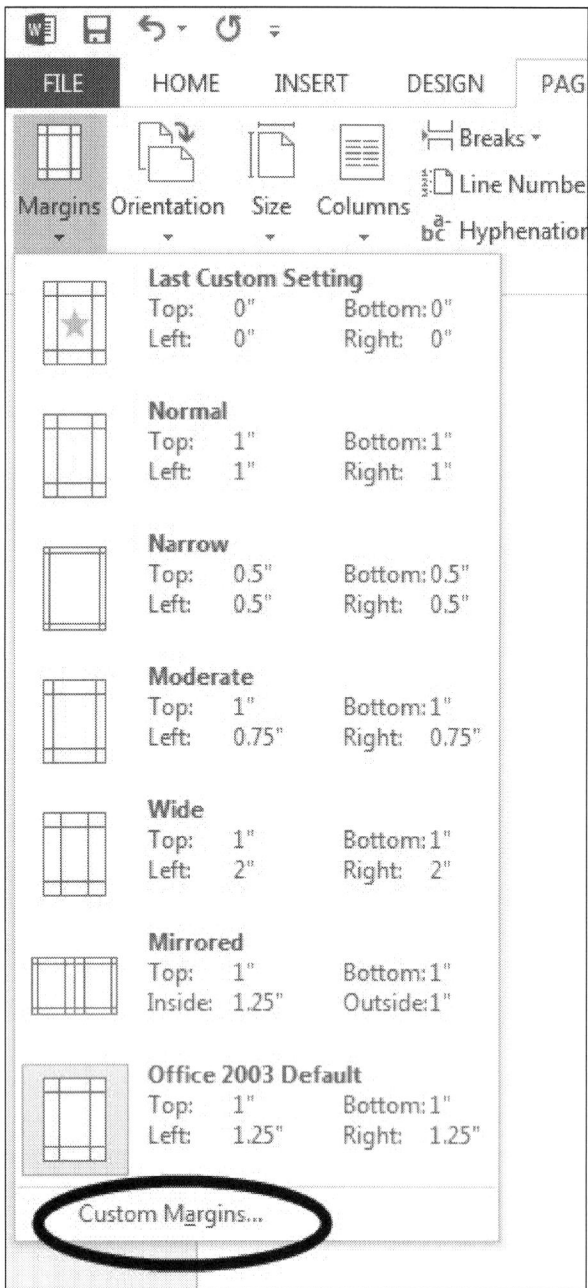

5. A Page Setup window will appear. (Another way to get this Page Setup menu is to click on the tiny arrow in the lower-right corner of the Page Setup rectangle):

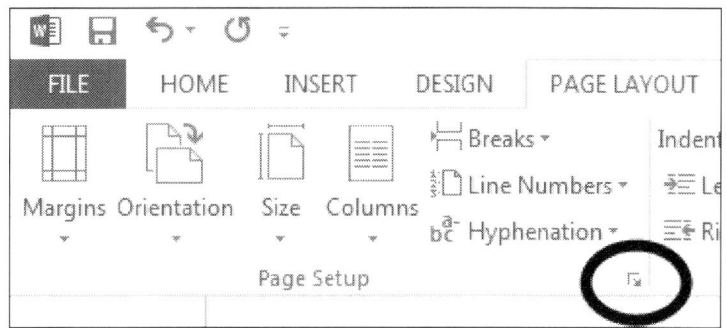

Here's what the Page Setup menu looks like:

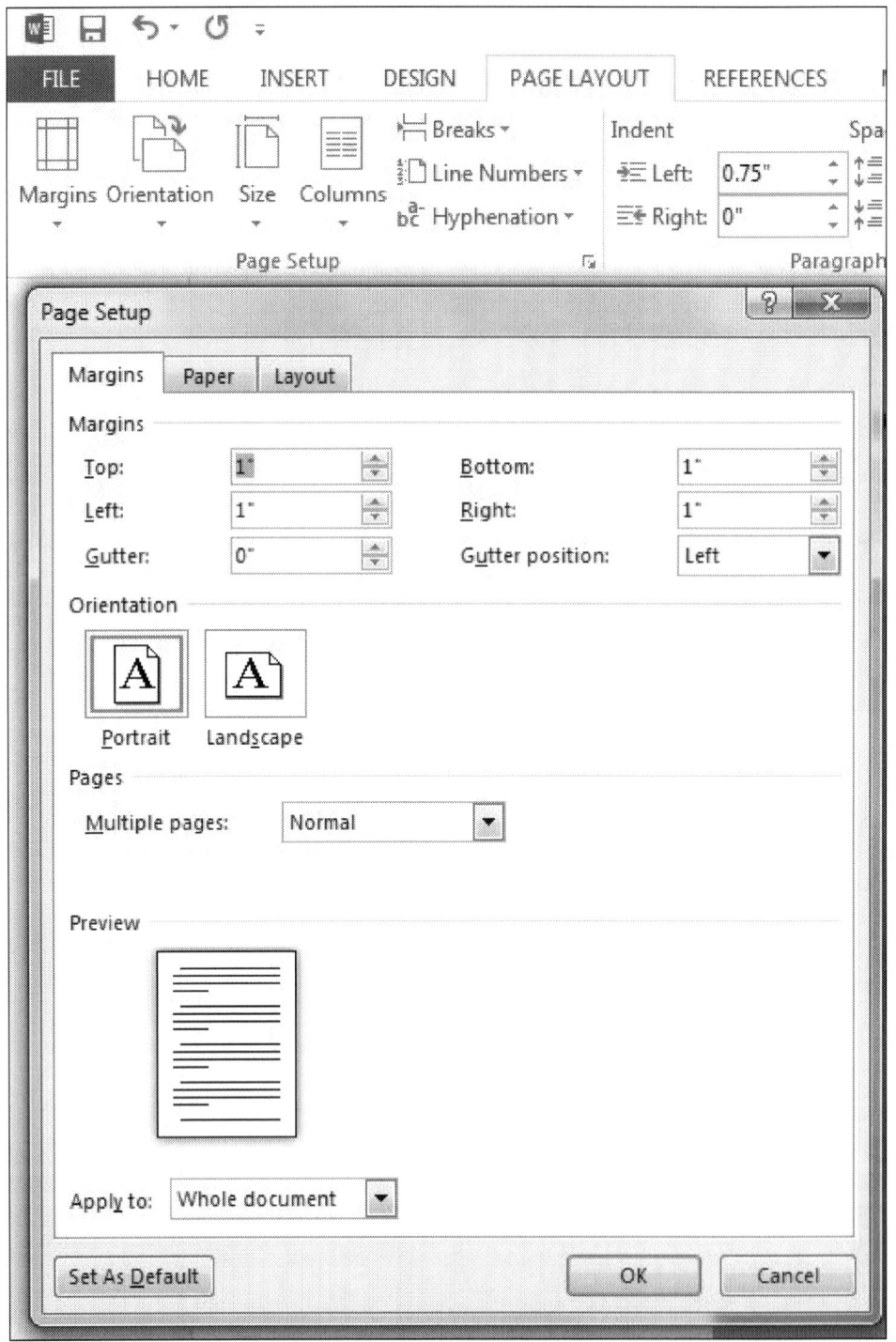

6. In the Page Setup menu, type in 1" for all four margins, and then click on "Set As Default" at the bottom of the window. Word will then ask you if you want to change the default settings. Click Yes. (If the "Yes" button is already highlighted, you can press the Enter key. If you want No, you can use the tab key to highlight No, and then press

Enter. Or you can press Esc to exit the dialogue box; that's the same as No.)

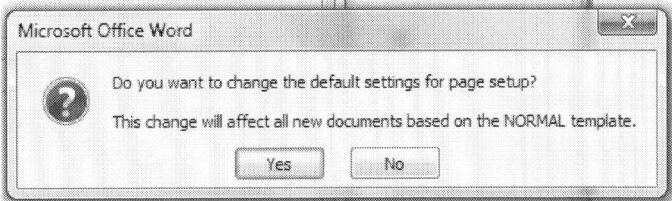

Page size

1. If you need to change your paper's page size (for example, if you want A4 size paper, which is standard in some countries), here's how. After clicking the Page Layout tab, then click on "Size":

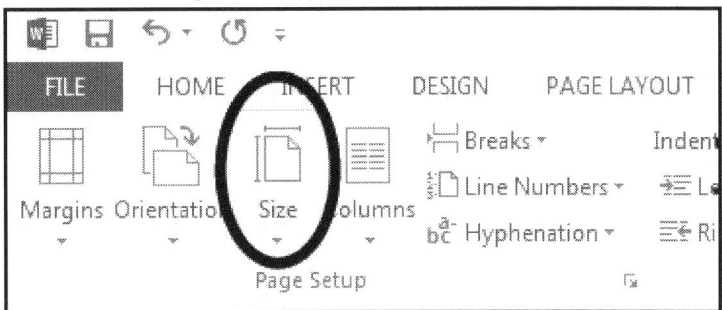

2. Click on "Letter" (or whatever size you want):

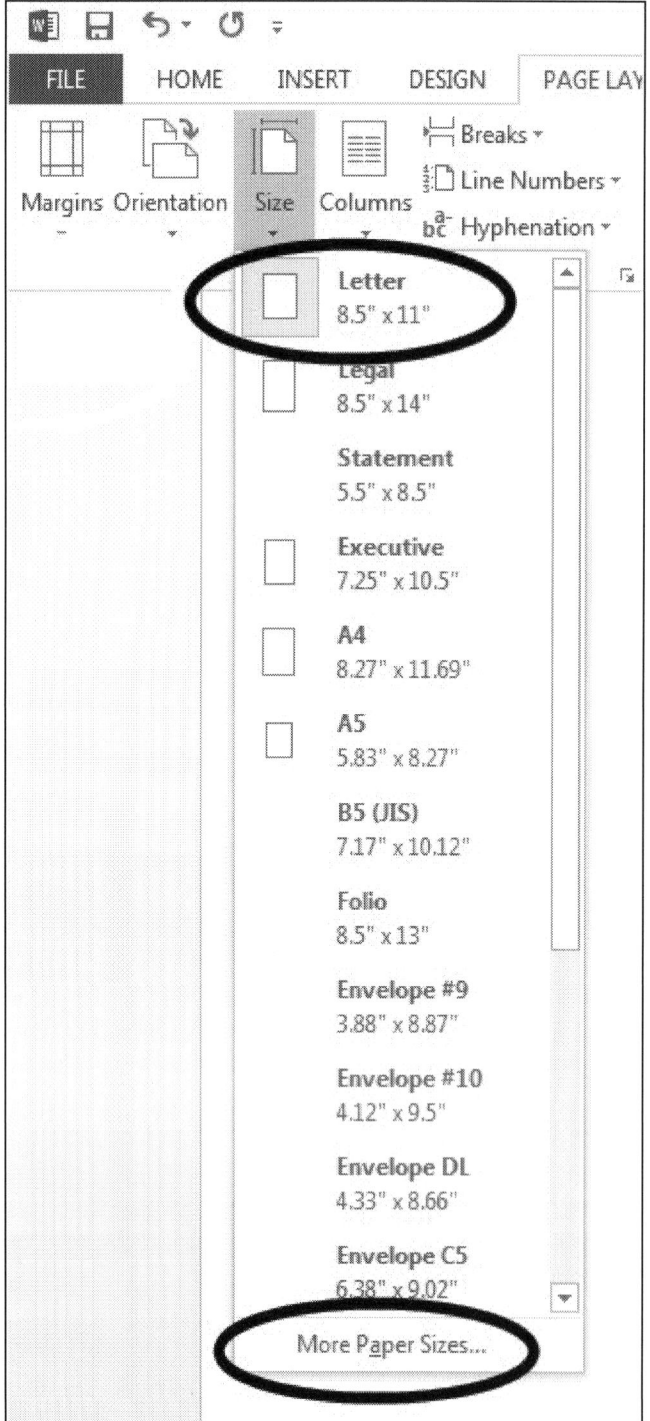

3. If you need to change your *default* paper size, click on "More Paper Sizes," shown above at the bottom of the drop-down menu.

4. A Page Setup Window will appear, with the "Paper" tab showing:

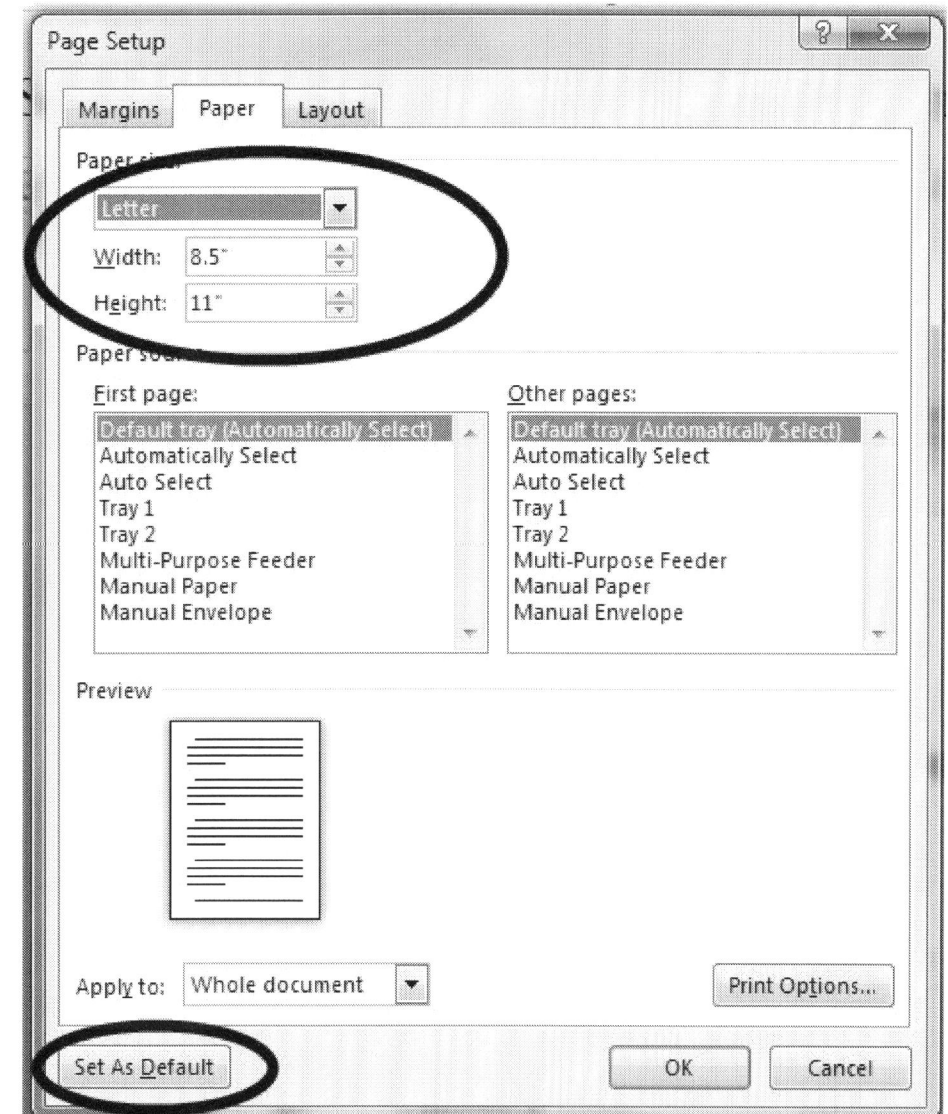

5. Type in the size of paper you want, and then click on "Set As Default." (Note that the D in Default is underlined. This indicates that you can also use the keyboard shortcut Alt-D. Other elements of the dialogue box also have underlined letters; these can be used with the Alt key if you prefer to navigate by using the keyboard rather than the mouse.) Just as with the change of margins, Word will ask you if you want to change the default. If so, click Yes.

Columns, breaks, header/footer options

Last, we will briefly mention some other items in the "Page Layout" menu:

- Orientation: For almost all purposes, use "Portrait." That is the default setting, so you shouldn't have to change it.

- Columns: Academic papers rarely use columns, so unless there is a special need, stick with the default of one column. Columns can be very useful for creating publications, but that is outside of the scope of this tutorial.

- Breaks: This is one way to cause the next line to start at the top of a new page. (The keyboard shortcut Ctrl-Enter also does this.) This can be useful if you want the works cited section (sometimes called a bibliography) to always start at the top of a new page. A page break is also useful for longer papers, such as a thesis, in which you have several chapters. Section breaks can be useful for longer papers, such as if you want a different header for different chapters of the paper.

  > (Many people put in extra paragraph returns (Enter) until they have forced the text to a new page. But if they later make edits to the text above and change the number of lines, then they have to go back and adjust the number of extra paragraph returns. Having an automatic page break simplifies this.)

- Line numbers: Don't use.

- Hyphenation: You may have the program hyphenate words at the end of a line, or you may leave automatic hyphenation off. Academic papers rarely use hyphenation.

- Headers and footers. There is a different place to *insert* a header or footer (text that automatically appears at the top or bottom of every page), but "Page Layout" is the place to control certain parts of the header or footer. Click on the tiny arrow at the lower right-hand corner of the Page Setup block:

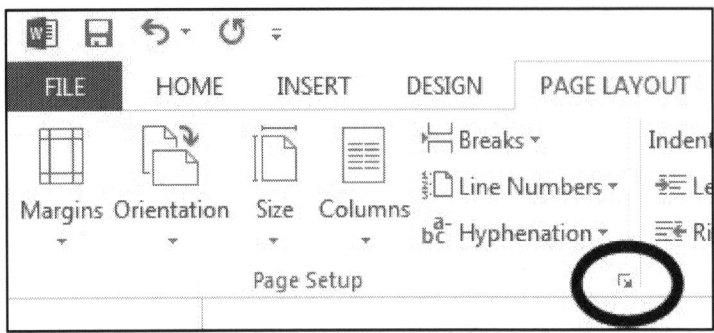

You will see a Page Setup window. Click on the Layout tab to see its menu:

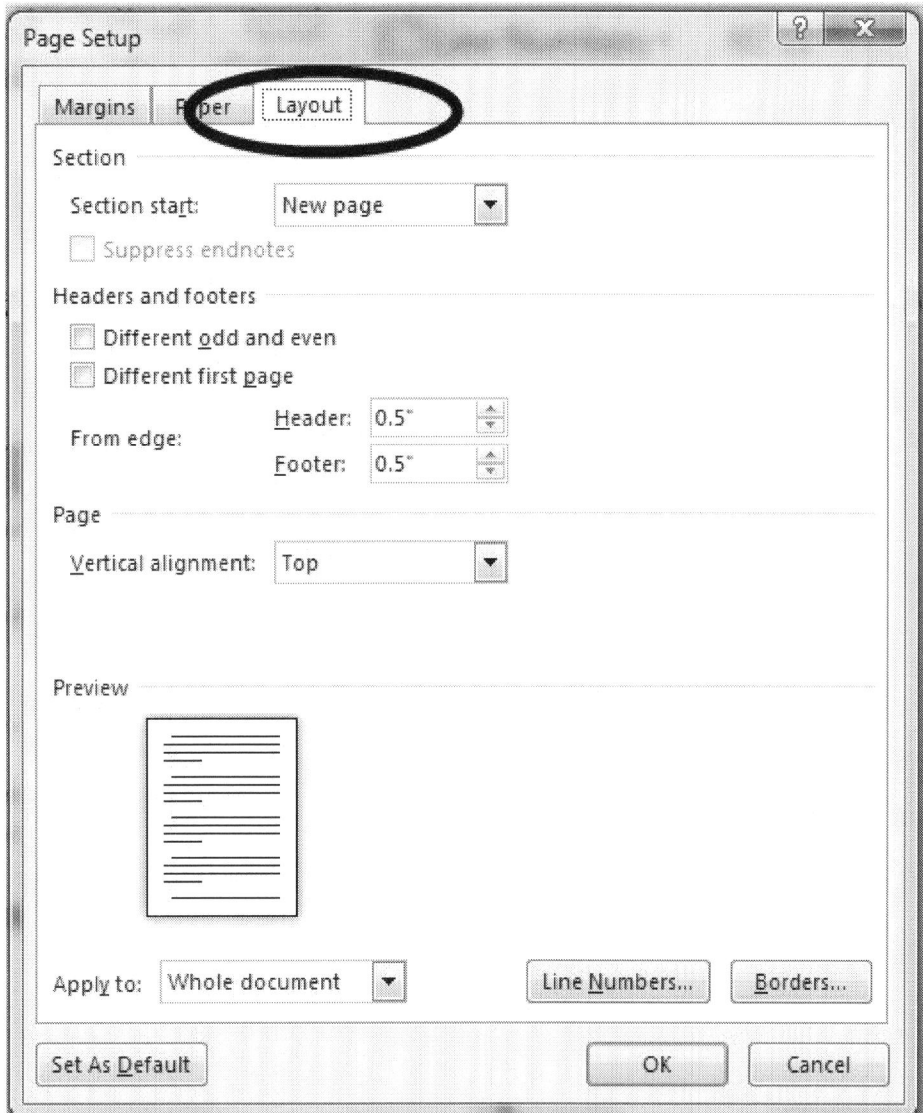

You can have a different header/footer on odd and even pages (appropriate for books, but not needed for academic papers).

- o You can have a different header/footer on the first page (this is how you can have NO header or footer on the first page).
- o You can change how far the header/footer is from the page edge.
- o You can center the text vertically in the middle of the page, but don't do this for an academic paper.
- o You can apply these settings to the entire document, to only this section (if you have broken your document into sections), or from this point forward.

- Also in the Page Layout menu ribbon: "Paragraph" settings. These are important, and complex. We will address those later.
- "Page Background" used to be part of the Page Layout ribbon, but it is now in the Design Menu. These options are useful for other documents, but are not needed for academic papers. With "Borders," you can put a border around your entire page. This might look good on a sheet of paper on a bulletin board, but it's not needed for an academic paper.

Font

When you first start Word, you will see the "Home" tab displayed. (It's called a tab because it looks a bit like a tab on a manila folder.) These tabs are very important to using Word, because each tab displays a different set of options. If the "Home" tab isn't displayed, click on the word "Home" and this is what you'll see:

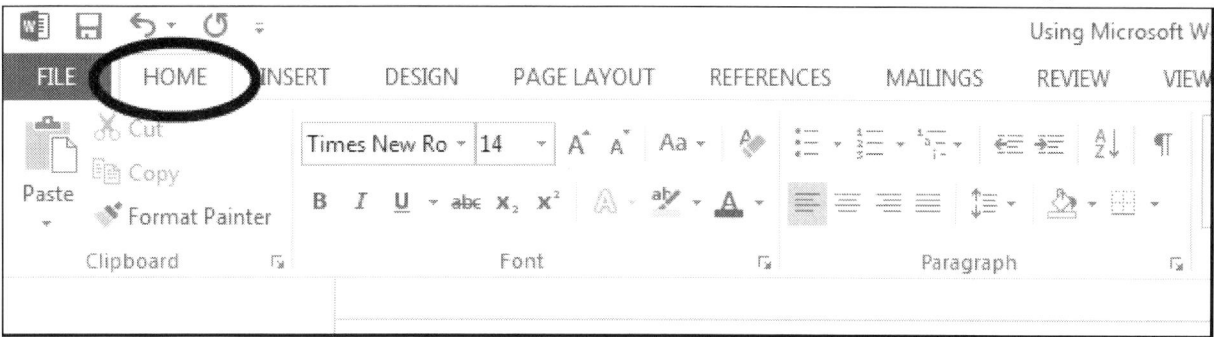

Let's focus now on the "Font" rectangle. It displays the font currently being used – in this case Times New Roman, which is a standard font for academic papers. This is the font used in many textbooks and newspapers, and some studies have shown that this is the easiest font to read when we have large amounts of text (as we do in an academic paper).

Changing the font

If you want to change the font, click on the small triangle to the right of "Times New Roman" (or whatever is displayed on your computer as the default):

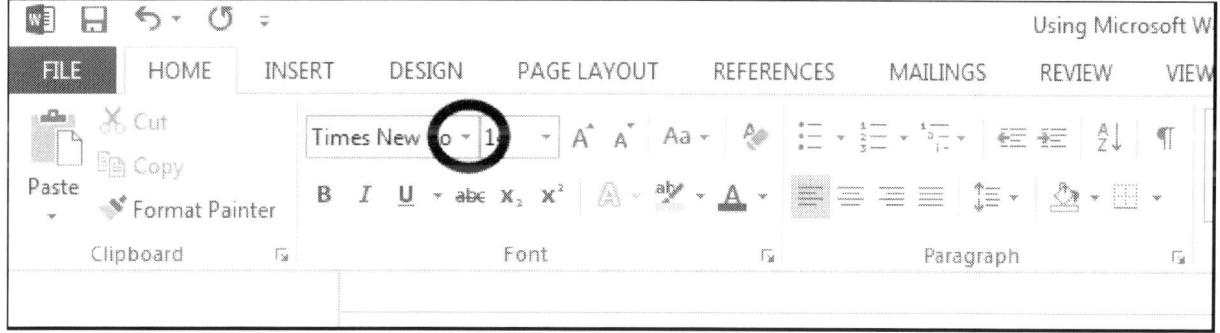

A drop-down menu will display a huge variety of options – the screen can show only about 10 percent of them. You can scroll down (using the mouse to drag the rectangle down the slide on the right-hand part of the drop-down box) to see more, or you can press a letter to jump to fonts starting with that particular letter. (If you want to see all the fonts starting with T, press U.)

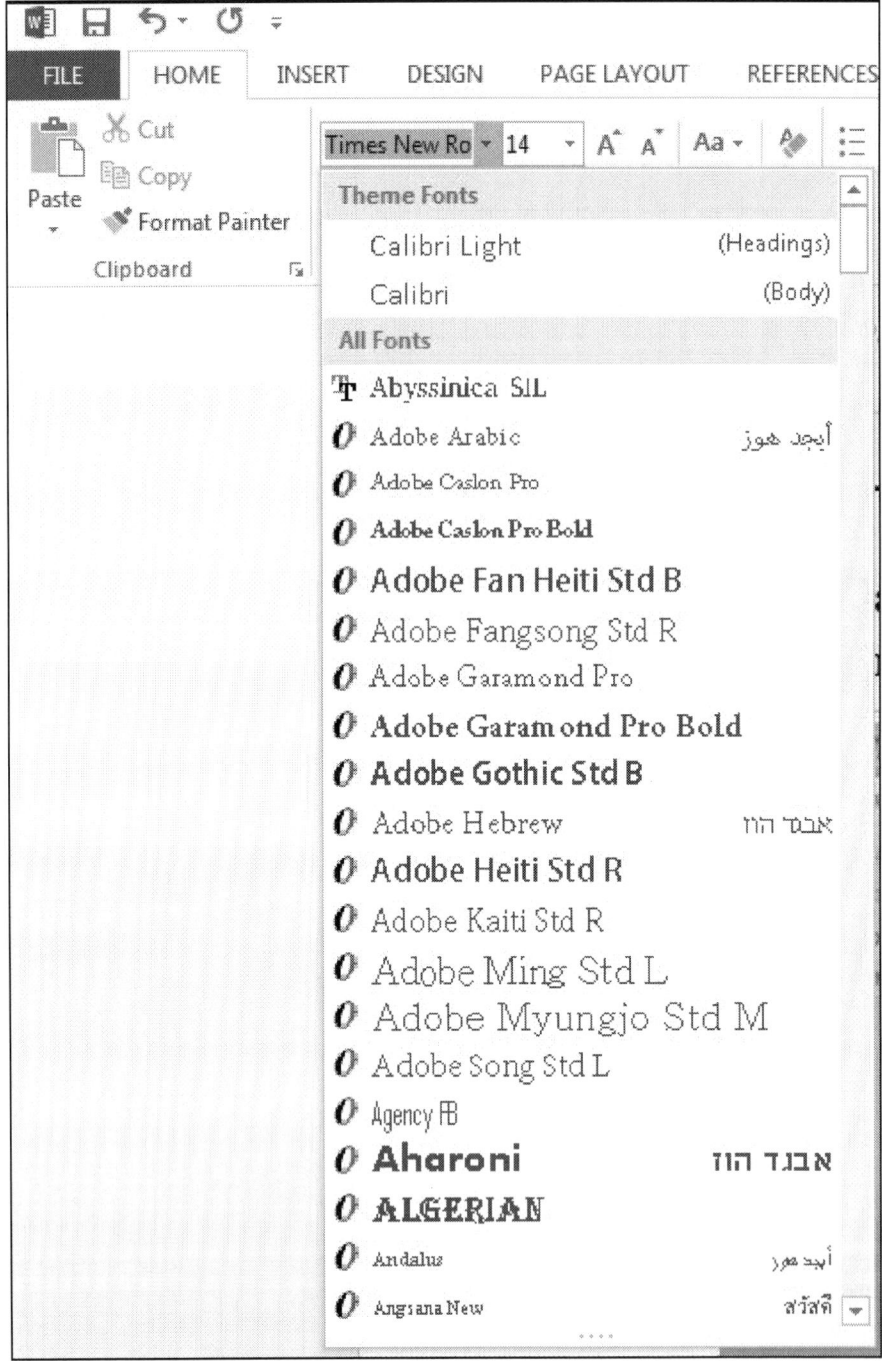

Calibri and Arial are common "sans-serif" fonts – fonts that are simple lines, without the tiny embellishments found on Times New Roman, Cambria, Book Antiqua and other "serif" fonts. To show you what a "serif" is, shown below is the letter A in Times New Roman, with one of the serifs circled, and in Arial:

Use fonts carefully. Too many font changes will make your paper look like a ransom note pasted together from newspaper advertisements. The basic rule is to use the same font for all of your main text – Times New Roman for most academic papers. You can use the same font for everything in your paper. If you really like variety, you can use a different font for subheads and captions. That's it. Keep it simple.

Pasting text from other documents

A problem arises when you copy electronic text – from a different document, the internet, or a software program. Sometimes the copied text will be in a different font, different size, or different style. There are two ways to deal with this problem.

For those who don't know, we will explain how to copy text from one program to another. In the other program (an internet browser such as Firefox, for example), put your mouse (or cursor) at the beginning of the text you want to copy. Then hold the left mouse button down while you move (or "drag") the mouse to the end of the text you want to copy. Let go of the button, and the text will be highlighted in a different color. In most programs, you can press the Ctrl key (Control) and the "c" key at the same time to copy that text into your computer's clipboard memory. (Or in many programs, you can click on "Edit" in the upper left, and then "Copy.") Then go to Word, put the mouse at the place you'd like the text to be, and press Ctrl and v at the same time. (The letter v was chosen because it looks like the proofreader's symbol for "insert something here." You can also click on the "Paste" icon at the left part of the Home ribbon.) The material is then inserted at that point. <u>Do not forget to use quote marks: all quoted text must be marked as a quote.</u>

1. After you have pasted the text, you can highlight it and manually change the font to what you want: Times New Roman, size 12. If you copy and paste frequently, this can be tedious, so you can wait until you have finished the paper, and then highlight the entire paper (press Ctrl and "a" at the time time), and then change the font for everything to Times New Roman 12.

A special problem occurs if you try to paste Hebrew, Greek or other non-Roman letters. This is usually a bad idea. If you are not familiar with those languages, you will have no idea of whether it is displayed correctly. If your instructor does not have the particular font you copied, then it will *not* be displayed correctly, and it will look like you don't know what you are doing. Transliteration into Roman characters is usually acceptable. If you need non-Roman characters, try to type it in Times New Roman (Use the "Insert" tab, then "Symbol" and "More Symbols.") If you use other characters frequently, ask your instructor about what font is preferred. If you use non-Roman fonts, then you do *not* want to highlight your entire paper and change the font for everything at once. You will have to be more selective.

2. When you paste something into Word, Word will give you an option for how it is to be pasted. The options are given in a small clipboard icon that comes at the end of the pasted material. For example:

lipboard icon that comes at

paste something

🗐 (Ctrl) ▾

If you hold your mouse over that icon, you will see what it's for – paste options:

If you click on the small triangle, or press Ctrl, you'll see the options:

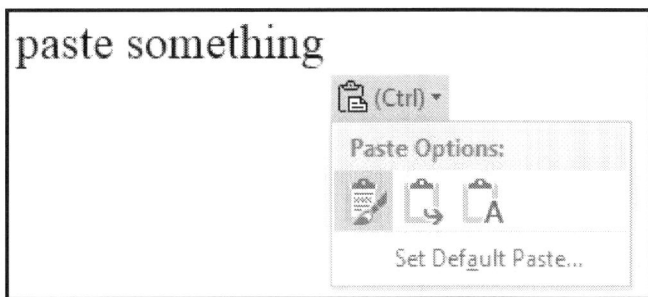

The option "Keep Source Formatting" is the one that usually gives you trouble. Choose one of the others. "Merge Formatting" is usually safe. "Keep Text Only" will eliminate all boldfacing and italics – sometimes you want to do that anyway. When you hold your mouse over the icons, you will also see some letters that are keyboard shortcuts, if you'd rather press a key than click a mouse. K will keep the source formatting, "m" will merge it into the format you are currently using in the document, and "t" will keep text only.

"Set Default Paste" is a way to set your preference for all future pasting. That takes you to a complicated screen:

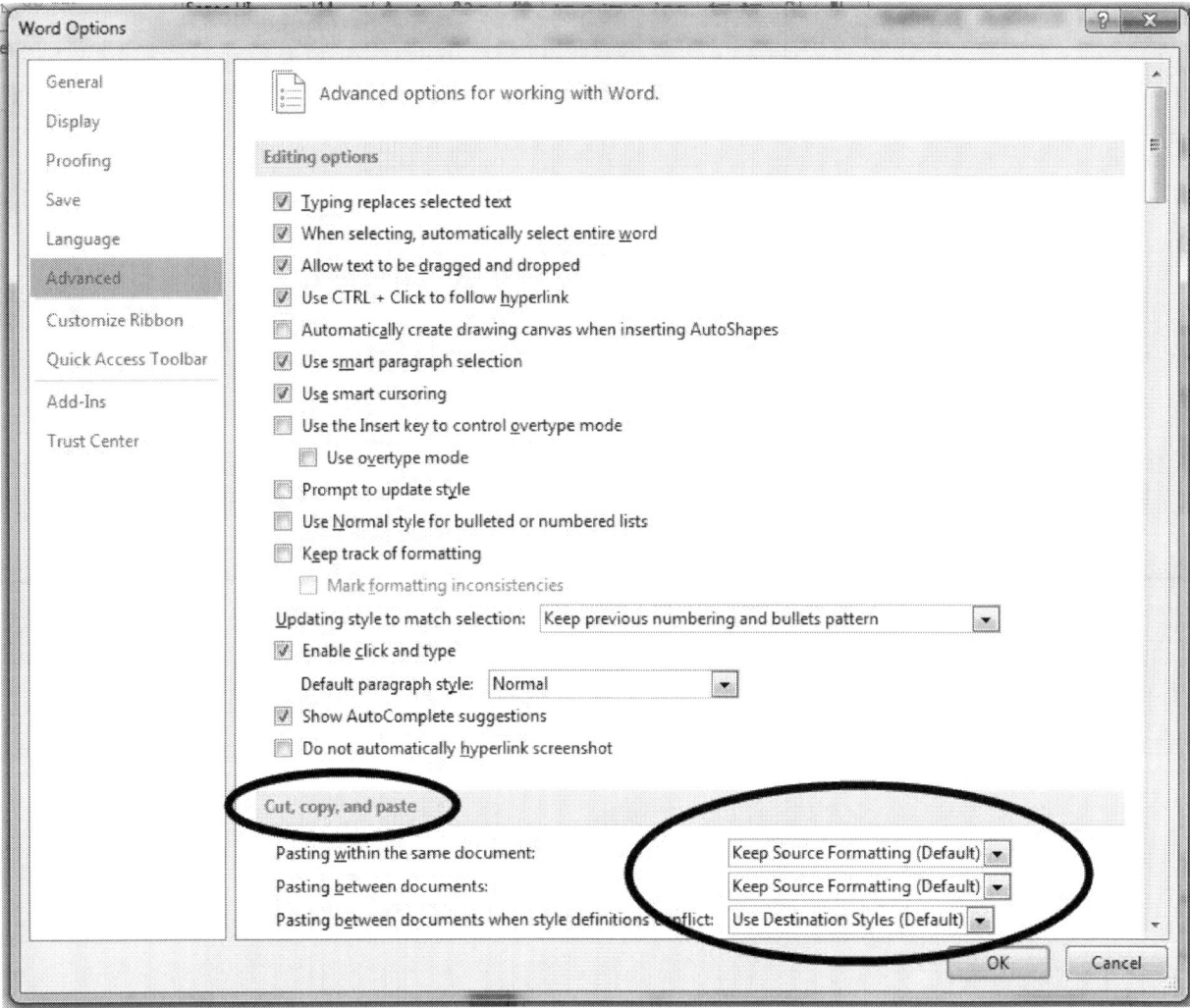

Under "Cut, copy, and paste," you can tell Word how you want it to handle material if it is copied from one part of the document to another, if it is copied from one Word document to another, or if it is copied from another program, such as an internet browser. In most cases, for academic papers, you want to match the destination formatting. Choose your options, and then click on "OK."

Even if you change your default for this, Word always gives you the option of changing it for a specific paste – just click on the little clipboard icon that appears right after you paste in some new text. Once you type more text or make any changes, that option disappears.

Changing font size

In the example shown below, you can see that the font is set to size 14:

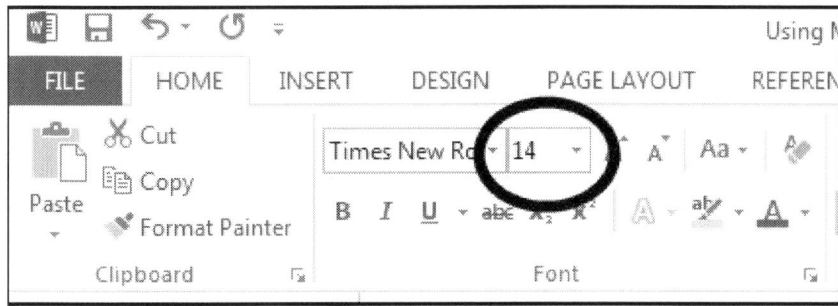

That's what we used for this document, because it's easier to read on a computer screen. But it is not the standard for academic papers, so you need to change it. There are at least four ways to do this (almost everything in Word can be done in more than one way):

1. Click on the "14" and type in your own number, such as 12. For academic papers, you want 12 in the main text. *Slightly* larger sizes, such as 14, can be used for titles, subheads, table captions, etc. Slightly smaller sizes can be used for footnotes. You can even type in half sizes, such as 10.5.

2. Click on the small triangle, and Word will display a number of choices. Click on 12.

3. To increase the font size, click (just to the right of area circled above) on the letter A with a triangle pointing upwards. That increases the font size by one for every click. Click on the A with a triangle pointing downward to decrease the size.

4. Press Ctrl and [at the same time to decrease the font, or Control and] to increase the font.

5. If you did this and nothing happened, that's probably because you hadn't selected any text. The font change will be implemented for the cursor, and for anything you type *after that point*. However, if you highlight some text first (by dragging the mouse over the text, or by double- or triple-clicking on the text), then the highlighted text will be changed. One click on the mouse puts your cursor at a certain point. Double-clicking the mouse will highlight one word. Triple-clicking the mouse will highlight the entire paragraph.

Other font attributes

Beneath the name of the font are icons for a number of other font attributes:

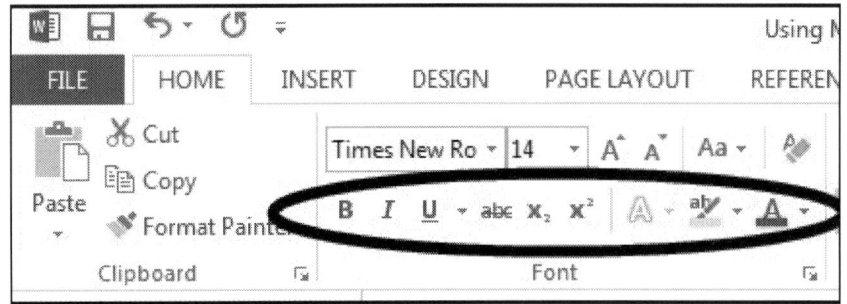

These are, from left to right: Bold, Italic, Underline, Strikethrough, Subscript, Superscript, Text Effects, Highlight, and Font Color. If you position your mouse over an icon for a couple of seconds, Word will display what each one of them does. It also displays a keyboard shortcut for some of them.

- For Bold, Ctrl-B or Ctrl-b (pressing Ctrl and b at the same time) will turn boldfacing on, or if it's already on, will turn it off. Boldfacing is appropriate for titles, subheads, section headings, and captions.

- Ctrl-I or Ctrl-i turns italics on and off. It is needed for book titles and non-English words, and can be used *sparingly* for emphasis. In academic papers, emphasis is usually achieved by your choice of words, not by variations in font. Don't litter your paragraphs with words in bold, italics, all caps, etc. You should use italics for titles of books, journals, magazines, movies, TV series, music albums, etc.

- Ctrl-U or Ctrl-u turns underlining on and off. Notice that there is a small triangle pointing downward to the right of the Underline icon. This lets you choose different styles of underlining – single, double, dashed, etc. But even single underlining is rarely needed in academic papers. In the days of typewriters, underlining was used to tell typesetters when to put a word in italics – that's how the custom of underlining book titles started. Now that ordinary people have the power of italics, underlining is no longer needed for this.

- Academic papers rarely need to ~~strike through~~ the text. Your instructor may wish to do it, but there's a better way to do it if it's needed for that purpose.

- Subscript is rarely needed unless you are typing chemical formulas.
- You rarely need to superscript anything, either. The most common use for superscripting is footnote numbering, and Word will do that automatically, if you use Word's feature for footnotes and endnotes.
- Text effects include outlines and shadows – artistic effects that are not needed for academic papers.
- You generally don't need to highlight anything in an academic paper, though your instructor may use that feature when making comments on your paper.
- You shouldn't change font color, either. Color is great for advertising flyers, but not for academic papers. If you have to express your flair and creativity, use very dark blue.
- There used to be an icon to change the capitalization style of highlighted text. It's gone now, but you can use the keyboard shortcut Alt-o, e). You can choose from Sentence case (only the first word capitalized), all lowercase, all caps, or every word capitalized.

The Font menu

Let's go back to the Font rectangle we started with, and notice the small arrow in the lower-right-hand corner:

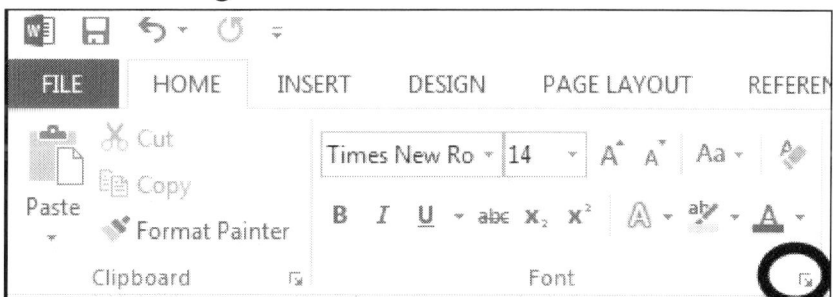

These little arrows are portals to something more complicated. If you click on that arrow, you'll get the Font menu (another way to get to the same menu is to Ctrl-d. Or press Alt-o, then f). Here's what you'll see:

This menu gives you yet one more way to change the font you are using, its size, and whether it is italic or bold, or both. There's another way to change color, underlining style, underlining color, and a variety of other special effects you should not use in an academic paper.

There's an underlined letter in each of the choices. This provides a keyboard shortcut for the options – only when this menu is displayed. In this menu, rather than pressing the letter you want (that will change the font), you need to press Alt and the letter at the same time. For example, Alt-p will turn superscripting on and off.

At the bottom left is the "Set As Default" button, by which you can make your changes effective for everything you do in the future. If your default font is not Times New Roman 12, you may want to change the font and size in this menu, and then click on "Default." If you commonly use a larger size of font, you may want to set it that way.

At the top of this menu is a tab labeled "Advanced." This is a portal into another part of the universe, in which words are either scrunched together or all spread out. You should not do this in an academic paper.

The Paragraph Menu

Paragraphs are a large part of a paper's format. Unfortunately, the default settings for Word are not designed for academic papers. The basic settings for academic papers should be: double-spaced, first line indented, left justified, and no extra space between paragraphs. Here's how to set it:

1. Right-click anywhere in a paragraph you'd like to change (or you can highlight more than one paragraph, and change them all at one time). (Right-click: use the button on the right-hand side of the mouse, instead of the one you usually use.) Right-clicking will generally give you a menu appropriate for the place you are. In this case it gives you two:

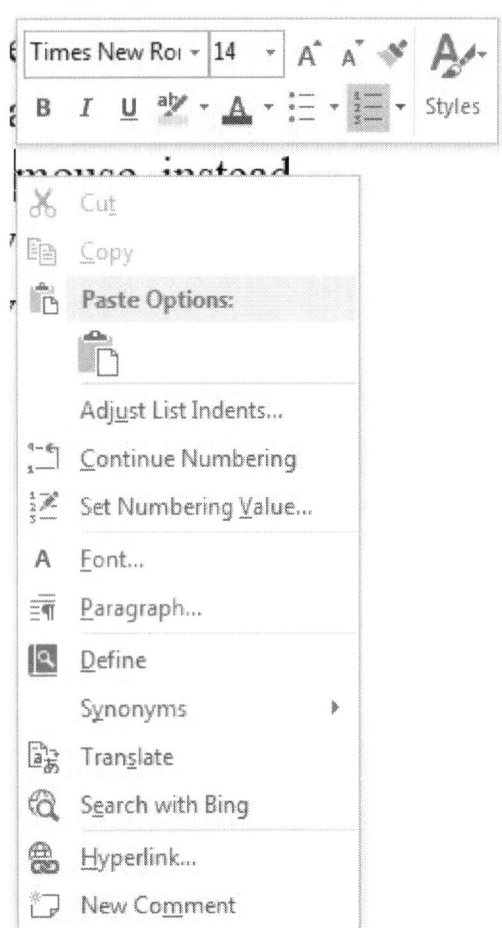

The top menu will change text, either what you have highlighted, or the word or paragraph.

2. To change the paragraph settings, click on "Paragraph" in the bottom menu. (There are two other ways to do steps 1 and 2:

a. Press Alt-o, then p. That will bring up the paragraph menu for whichever paragraph the cursor is in.

b. Another way is to click on the small arrow in the lower-right-hand corner of the "Paragraph" box in the "Home" tab.)

Here's the menu:

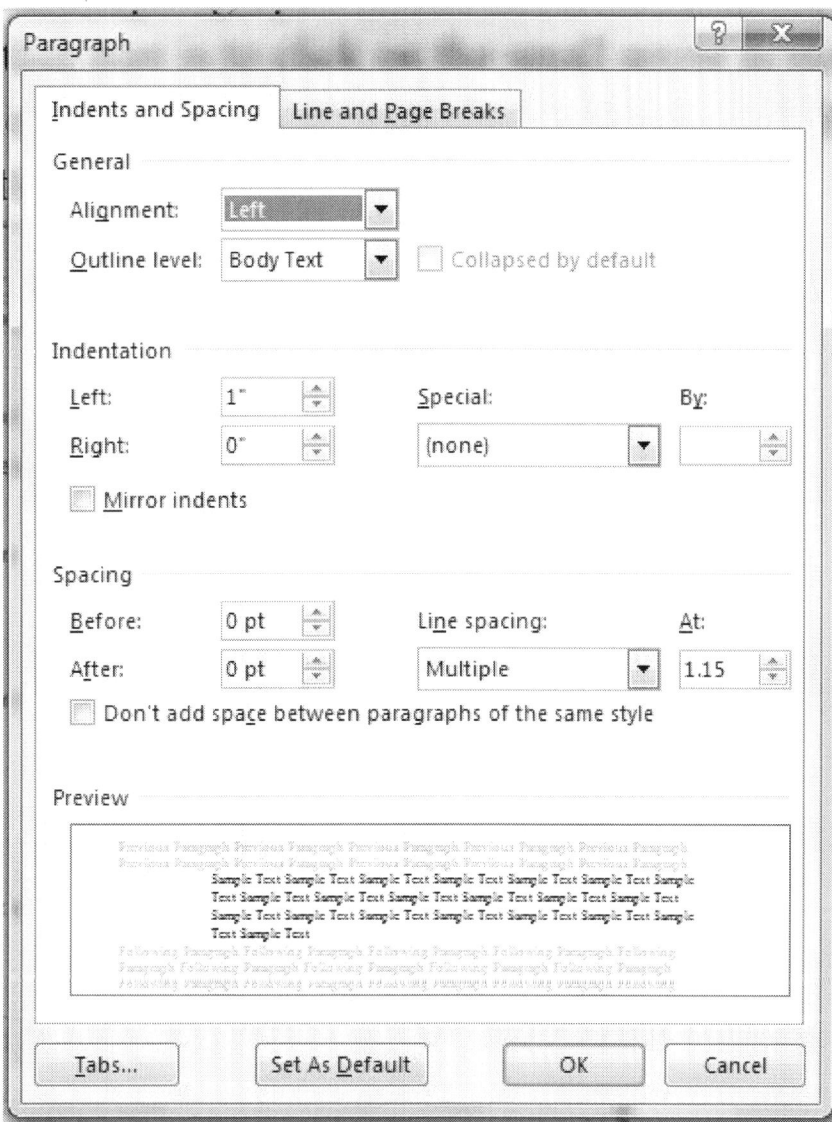

There is a lot packed into this menu.

a. Alignment: set it to Left.

- "Centered" is OK for the title of your paper, but not for the main text.
- "Right" aligns the right-hand side but leaves the left uneven (or ragged).

- "Justified" aligns both left and right columns. This can sometimes make the text hard to read because Word expands words and spaces in order to achieve that alignment.

b. Outline level: Leave it at Body text. The other choices refer to multi-level outlines, which we will briefly address below.

c. Indentation: Set left and right at zero. The primary exception to this is if you have a long quote, five lines or more. They should be a separate paragraph, indented an extra amount.

d. Special: Choose "First line," and set it at half an inch. That means the first line will be indented. This means that it is not necessary to type the tab character at the beginning of each paragraph. (If you already have some text, and put your cursor at the beginning of the first line and press Tab, Word will automatically transform that Tab into an indent in the paragraph format.)

e. Spacing: Set both before and after to zero. Word's default puts in an extra ten points after each paragraph. This may be good for business letters, but it's wrong for academic papers.

f. Line spacing: Choose "Double." This means you do not have to hit Enter twice at the end of every line, like people had to do with manual typewriters. You have to hit Enter only at the end of a paragraph. A keyboard shortcut for double-spacing when your cursor is in the paragraph: Ctrl-2. (Academic papers are almost always double spaced. If you want to single space a document, the lines are often a bit close to one another. Line spacing 1.1 or 1.15 looks better. Choose Line Spacing Multiple, then type what you want. Or you can also specify a minimum distance.)

g. If you click on the "Line and Page Breaks" tab (or if you are already in the Paragraph menu, you can use the keyboard shortcut

Alt-p), you'll see part 2 of the Paragraph menu:

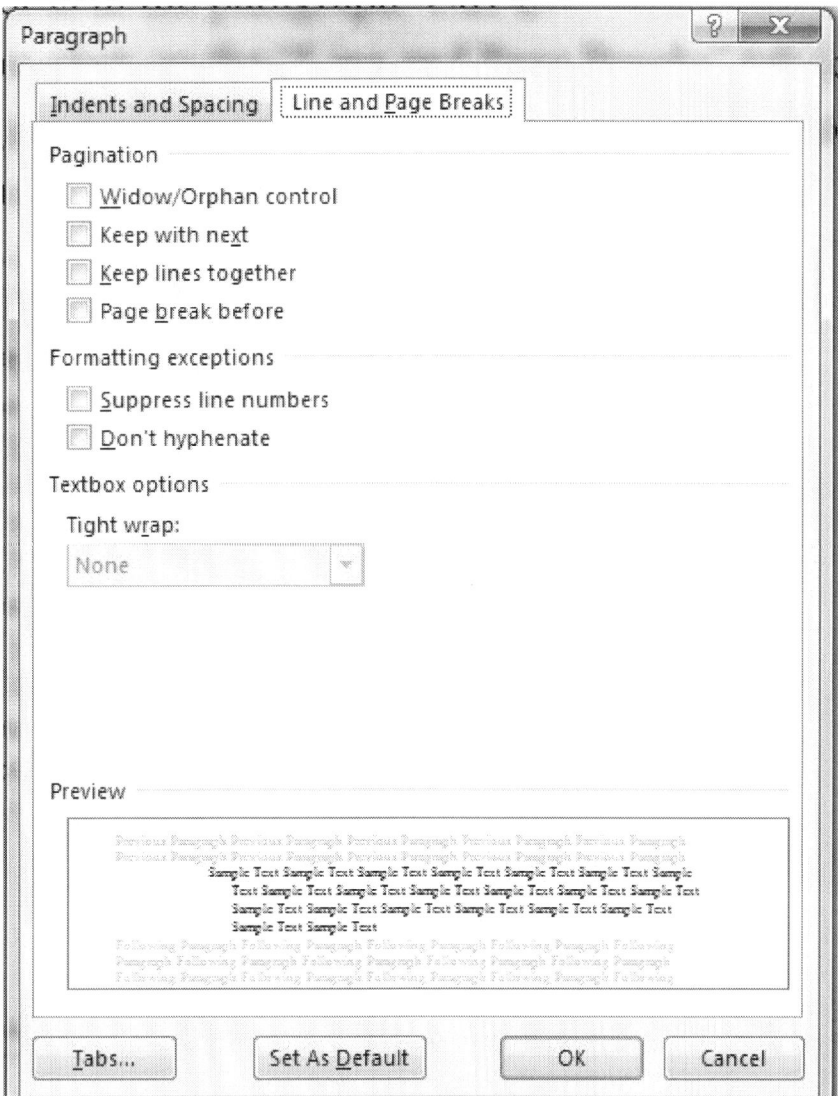

h. "Widow/Orphan control" refers to lines at the beginning or end of a paragraph. If only one line of the paragraph is on one page, and the rest is on another page, you have an orphan or a widow, depending on whether it's the first line or the last line. This is important in typesetting books, less important for academic papers, and even less important when those papers are viewed on a computer screen. Either setting is OK for academic papers. (If widow/orphan is checked, sometimes paragraphs will jump around from one page to another as you are typing near a page break. It doesn't hurt anything, but this might explain Word's sometimes inexplicable behavior.)

i. "Keep with next" is useful for subheads, or section headings. It prevents the subhead from being at the bottom of the page, by itself, while the body text is on the next page.

j. "Keep lines together" will prevent the entire paragraph from being separated, part on one page and part on another. In most paragraphs, this does not matter, so don't check this box.

k. "Page break before" is one way to ensure that your "Works Cited" section always begins at the top of a page. Another way to achieve the same goal is to insert a manual page break (mentioned in our discussion of Page Format). One practical difference in these two methods is that the manual page break can be seen when you reveal hidden characters, but the "page break before" setting can't be seen.

l. Click "Tabs" if you want to change the tab settings. Most papers don't need tabs at all, or work well with the default settings, so we won't go into those details.

m. "Set as Default" will change this for everything you type in the future. This can also be done by using Styles. We cover that later.

n. Click OK to save your changes for this paragraph (or all the paragraphs you have highlighted ahead of time).

3. If you hit Enter at the end of this paragraph, the next paragraph will be formatted exactly as this one is. So if you set your first paragraph correctly, the others will be OK, too.

4. Another way to get other paragraphs to be like this one: Use "Format Painter." Triple-click in one paragraph to highlight the entire paragraph. Then click on "Format Painter" in the upper left corner of the Home ribbon – the icon is a paintbrush:

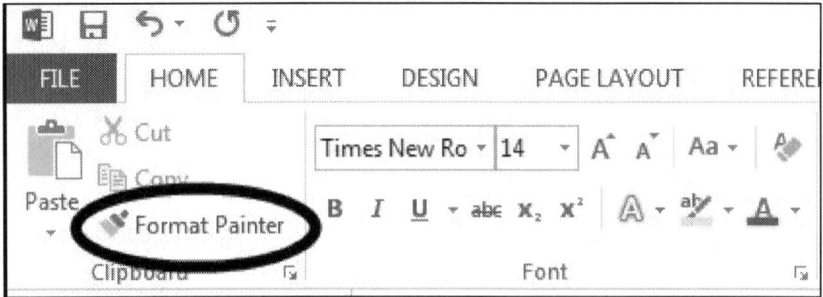

Your next click will transform whatever paragraph you click in, so that it is formatted like the source paragraph. If you first *double*-click on the Format Painter, you can click to change as many paragraphs as you want, until you hit Escape or some other menu item.

Hidden paragraph codes

This section is a bit technical, and it's not really about academic papers. But it is about one of the quirks of Word that sometimes cause us frustration.

1. Sometimes when you copy or move text, you are also copying the paragraph codes. You can't always *see* whether you are copying those codes, and the result is sometimes one way, sometimes another. If all your paragraphs are of the same formatting, this doesn't matter much. But if you are copying from one type of paragraph to another, this can result in changes that you didn't ask for. This can be frustrating.

2. The codes for the paragraph appear to be stored at the *end* of the paragraph. This paragraph does not have a blank space at the end, but if you triple-click to highlight the entire paragraph, it *looks* like it has a blank space at the end:

> 2. The codes for the paragraph appear to be stored at the *end* of the paragraph. This paragraph does not have a blank space at the end, but if you triple-click to highlight the entire paragraph, it *looks* like it has a blank space at the end:

That empty space represents the hidden paragraph code. To illustrate this, let's highlight just the last line of the paragraph – put the cursor in front of "blank" and press Shift-End. That's a keyboard shortcut for highlighting everything to the end of a line. The result is:

> blank space at the end:

Note that the highlighted area includes a blank space at the end, even though there *is* no space there. This seems to hold the paragraph code. Now let's boldface the area we have highlighted (Ctrl-b). Word not only boldfaces the text we highlighted, but (because this is an automatically numbered paragraph) it also boldfaces the initial, automatically-supplied number for the paragraph – the 2:

> **2.** The codes for the paragraph appear to be stored at the *end* of the paragraph. This paragraph does not have a blank space at the end, but if you triple-click to highlight the entire paragraph, it *looks* like it has a **blank space at the end:**

So, by boldfacing the "non-space" at the end of the paragraph, we have affected the start of the paragraph. However, we get a different result if we highlight that last line in a slightly different manner. As before, position the cursor in front of "blank" and press Shift-End to highlight the entire line. Then press Shift-Left Arrow (←), and the "non-space" at the end of the paragraph will no longer be highlighted:

blank space at the end:

Now if we boldface the highlighted text, only the text we selected is highlighted; the initial paragraph character is not. This shows us that the hidden "non-space" at the end of the paragraph contains codes that affect the paragraph. It might also explain why, in a numbered list, the numbers are occasionally in a different font than the rest of the paragraph. Word hides the codes, so sometimes it's hard to tell what you are doing.

3. Now let's see how this works in another setting. Suppose you have three different paragraphs – different fonts, sizes and indents:

Subhead

1. Numbered list

Ordinary paragraph

Let's highlight the second paragraph with a triple-click:

Subhead

1. Numbered list

Ordinary paragraph

Note that the "non-space" at the end of the paragraph is also highlighted. Then we copy (Ctrl-C) that text, move our cursor to the end of the first paragraph, and paste (Ctrl-V) the text.

1. **Subhead** Numbered list

2. Numbered list
Ordinary paragraph

Word has given us a hybrid of the two paragraphs. Because we copied and pasted the hidden paragraph code, it has turned the first paragraph into a numbered paragraph, indented the same as the second, and it has included an extra paragraph return we didn't ask for. But the original fonts are retained.

How can we prevent this problem? By being careful to *not* highlight the "non-space" at the end of the paragraph. After triple-clicking, press Shift-Left Arrow to un-highlight the paragraph code space at the end of the paragraph.

When you highlight text by dragging the mouse, Word will often highlight the paragraph code when you include the last character in the paragraph (a period, in this case). If you move the cursor carefully, you can unselect that space. You can also use the keyboard to highlight the text. Put your cursor where you wish to start, hold down the Shift key and press the Right Arrow key until you have highlighted the text you want.

Paragraph Icons

Let's look at the icons that Word has in the Paragraph section of the Home tab:

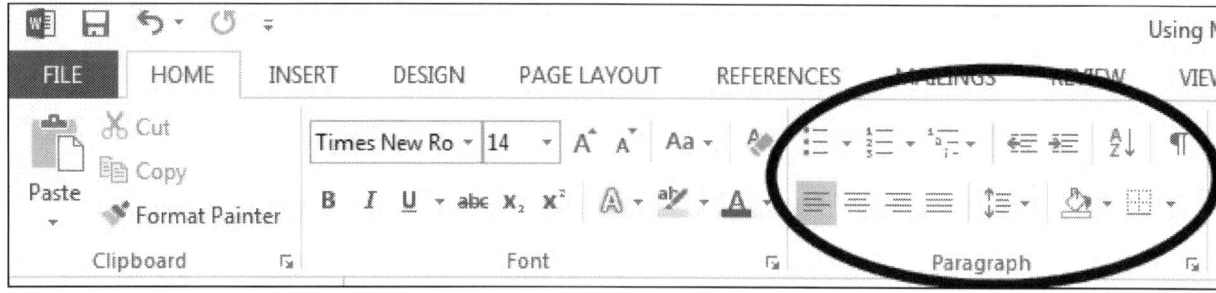

The first three icons can add structure to your paragraph:

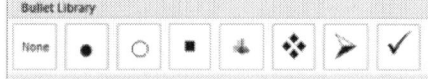

- The first one adds "bullets" (solid circles) at the beginning of your paragraph (this paragraph is an example). It also automatically indents all the subsequent lines in your paragraph. This can be an effective way to highlight supporting points or other items. (Like most formatting options, it should be used sparingly, because it can look choppy.) If you click on the small triangle to the right of the icon, you will see some choices for what that introductory character will be:

You can use additional characters if you wish, but in academic papers it's best to keep your formatting simple.

In its default setting, Word will automatically create a bulleted paragraph if you begin a paragraph with an asterisk and a space. If you hit Enter at the end of a bulleted paragraph, it will automatically create another bulleted paragraph. If you are done with bulleting, hit Enter again, or click on the Bullets icon in the Home ribbon to stop it. (Another way to turn an ordinary paragraph into a bullet paragraph is to press Ctrl-Shift-L.)

2. The second icon is for a numbered list (this paragraph is an example). The number is "hanging" out to the left, and all the subsequent lines are indented. The first paragraph will be

numbered 1. If you hit Enter at the end of the paragraph, Word will automatically begin a paragraph starting with 2, and so forth. If you are done with your list, click on the "Numbering" icon to stop it, or hit Enter again.

This type of list is appropriate for items in which the order is important. For example, in this paper we use it for steps in a sequence. Do number one first, then number two, etc. If you need to move paragraphs up or down, Word will automatically renumber them. That's a nice feature.

The small triangle to the right of the "Numbering" icon gives you options on the numbers: Arabic numerals, Roman numbers, capitalized, lower-case, and so forth. Usually the default is good enough. In its default setting, Word will automatically create a numbered paragraph if you begin the paragraph with 1, I, I, A or "a" followed by a period or a closing parenthesis:) and a space. If Word does this and you don't want it to, you can correct it by means of Undo (Ctrl-Z) or by

clicking the AutoCorrect icon that appears when Word changes your formatting. We'll say more about AutoCorrect later.

3. The third icon in the Paragraph box is for a Multilevel List. This is for complex outlines. There are options for how to alternate between Roman and Arabic numbers, capital and lower-case letters, how much to indent the number, how much to indent the text, and what fonts to use. Academic papers rarely need these features, and they are complex, so we won't address all the details.

a. The easiest way to create a multi-level list or outline is to start with a numbered list. At the end of the paragraph, hit Enter. Word will automatically supply a new numbered paragraph with the next higher number. If you now hit the Tab key, Word will then indent the paragraph further and start a new type of numbering. That's how we created this paragraph, which begins with "a." Or you can change the level later, by positioning the cursor at the beginning of a line, and pressing Tab. The entire paragraph will be indented and put into a new numbering scheme.

b. Normally you should not have a 1 without a 2, nor an "a" without a "b." There is no need to "divide" something into only one subpoint.

    i. You rarely need more than two levels of an outline, but to illustrate a third level, we formed this paragraph by hitting Enter and then Tab again. It indents the paragraph yet further and starts a new list. This can get complicated, and very few academic papers need it. It can also be frustrating for Word to do this re-formatting if you didn't want it to. So it's best to keep it simple.

4. What if you don't like the placement of your bulleted or numbered list? Perhaps it is indented too far, or the number is too far away from the text. Sometimes it's best to leave well enough alone. But if you'd like to change it, and are up to the challenge, you can.

a. Click on the initial bullet, number or letter, and it will be highlighted:

> 4. What if you d
> list? Perhaps

b. Right-click on the highlighted character and you'll see these menus:

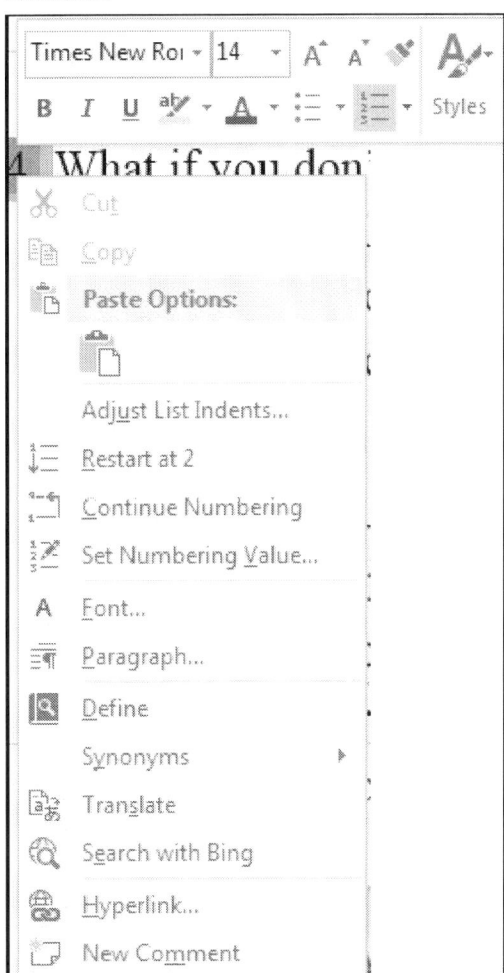

c. The top menu is for the font – you can use a different font or size for the initial character if you wish.

d. You can continue numbering from a previous list (if you have intervening paragraphs without numbers, Word won't automatically know that this one is in the same series), or you can set a new numbering value, and start at the number 5, if for some reason you want to.

e. You can decrease or increase the indent. That moves the entire paragraph to left or right (and it may change the initial character, too, just as the Tab key does).

f. If you want to adjust the *relative* indentation of the initial character as compared with the main text, you need to click on "Adjust List Indents" (the letter u is underlined, showing that the shortcut key is u). This is the menu you'll see:

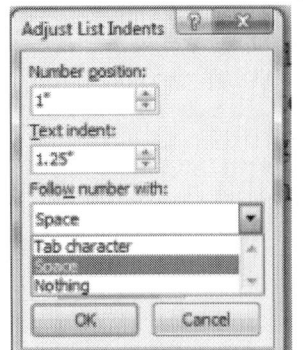

    g. Here you can make exact adjustments for where the initial character is, where the main text is, and what comes between the initial character and the text. You may need some experimentation to see what looks best. Remember: sometimes it's best to leave well enough alone. This can be tricky.

Indent left and right, sort, show codes

The next four icons in the paragraph box control other functions. As usual, positioning your mouse over the icon for a couple of seconds will show you what each is for.

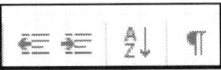

1. "Decrease indent" moves the entire paragraph (not just the first line) to the left, usually by one-half inch. (Pressing Shift-Tab will do the same thing, if the cursor is at the beginning of any of the lines.) If the paragraph is already at the margin, this won't work. If you want the paragraph to display left of the margin, you can use the paragraph menu (Alt-o, p) and type in a negative number for left indentation.

2. "Increase indent" moves ordinary paragraphs to the right a half inch. For bulleted lists, it will move the paragraph to the right *and* change the style of bullet. (Pressing Tab will do the same thing, if the cursor is at the beginning of any of the lines.) For numbered lists, it will move everything to the right and change the style of numbering, in the way that is controlled by the multi-level list setup. That is too complicated for this tutorial, because you don't have much need for it in academic papers.

3. "Sort" allows you to put your paragraphs in alphabetic order. This can be useful in your Works Cited section, since bibliographic entries there should

be in alphabetical order. Make sure you highlight only the paragraphs you wish to be alphabetized – for example, do not include your section heading in the highlight. If you use use three dashes (———) to indicate "same author as above," it will not alphabetize them correctly.

4. The "Show/Hide" icon – the backwards P (¶) is a typesetter's sign for paragraph – will show you *some* of Word's codes. It will display a tiny dot for each space, and the backwards P at the end of every paragraph. It will also mark tab spaces, page breaks, non-breaking spaces, non-breaking hyphens, optional hyphens, a manual line break, and a few other characters you probably don't use. This can sometimes be helpful in troubleshooting formatting difficulties.

Paragraph justification

The first four icons in the second row are for paragraph justification. These can also be set in the Paragraph menu, but Word provides icons for them, too:

1. Align Text Left makes the left edges of the paragraph straight, the right edge ragged. This is recommended for academic papers, since it is easier to read, because spacing between letters and words is consistent.

2. Center (Ctrl-e) is useful for titles, sometimes section headings, and graphics. But for Word, "center" does not always mean center of the page – it centers text after taking into allowance any first line or paragraph indents. If you want something to be truly centered, you need to use the paragraph menu to remove all such indents. You can remove some indents by positioning the cursor at the beginning of the paragraph, then pressing Backspace until the text is touching the left margin. Then press Ctrl-e to center the paragraph.

3. Align Text Right gives you a ragged left edge, straight right edge. This can be useful to imitate a signature at the end of a special block of text, but this is not recommended for academic papers.

4. Justify will make both left and right margins straight. Word does this by adding space between words and letters. Either Ctrl-j or Ctrl-l (the L key, but not with the shift) will toggle between left justified and both margins justified.

Line spacing, shading, and borders

There is rarely a need for the last three icons, especially the last two:

1. The first one controls line spacing. If you click on the small triangle, you'll get a menu:

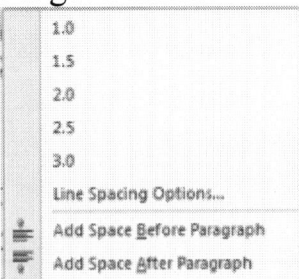

   This presents a choice of spacing: single spacing, 1.5 line spacing, double spacing, triple spacing. The keyboard shortcuts for these are Ctrl-1, Ctrl-5, Ctrl-2, and there is no shortcut for triple spacing. Line Spacing Options takes you to the Paragraph menu. Add Space Before Paragraph adds an extra 12 points (about one line) above the paragraph; Add space After Paragraph adds 12 points below. These are rarely needed, because when you want to make such adjustments you usually want to adjust other details as well, so it is better done in the paragraph menu.

2. Shading, when a low percentage is used, can highlight a paragraph, or a row in a table. This is rarely needed in academic papers.

3. The last icon is for Border. You can put borders around words, paragraphs, or whatever you have highlighted. This is rarely needed in academic papers.

Styles

Styles are one of the most complicated and powerful tools that Word has. After you learn how to use them, some tasks in Word will be easier. We'll show you enough to get you started. First, note the Styles section on the right half of the Home tab:

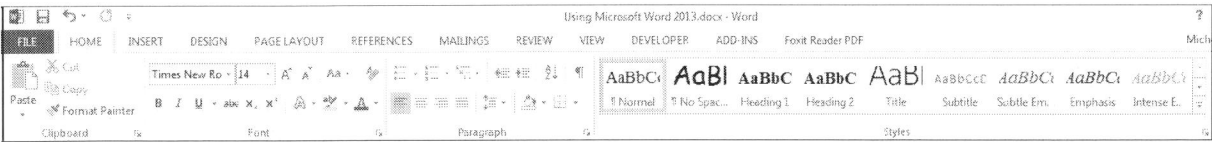

Now let's zoom in on the Styles section:

The number of styles shown will depend in part on the size of your computer monitor, or the window you are using. But if you click on the small triangle (circled above), you'll see more styles to choose from:

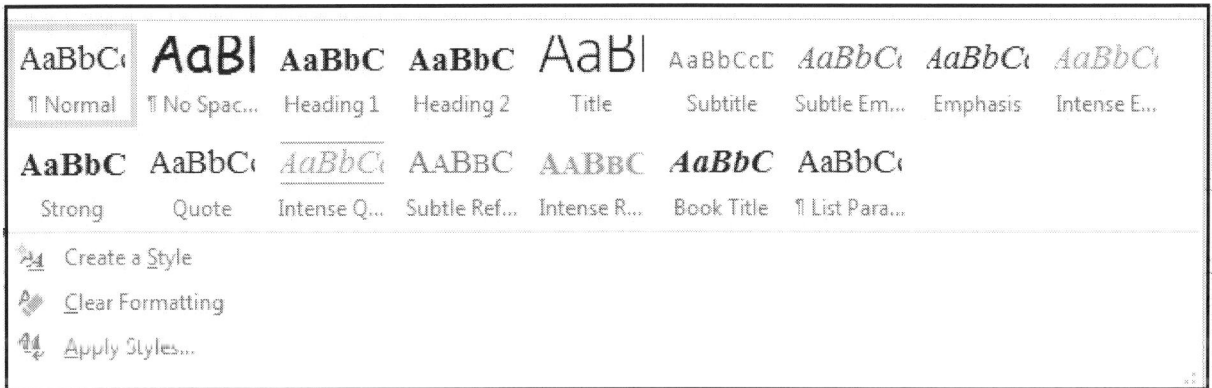

The light blue border around the "Normal" style shows that it's the one currently being used – the one your cursor is in. If you position your mouse over another style, such as "Heading 1," then you will see what your paragraph would look like in this style. In some cases massive reformatting will be displayed. Don't worry – your document will not be changed unless you *click* on that style. If you click on a style, you will change whatever paragraph your cursor is in.

Changing the Normal style

"Normal" is the default style that begins whenever you start a new document. It is also the style that several other styles are based on. Change this style and you can make your experience with Word easier.

If you right-click on the name of the style, you will get a small menu:

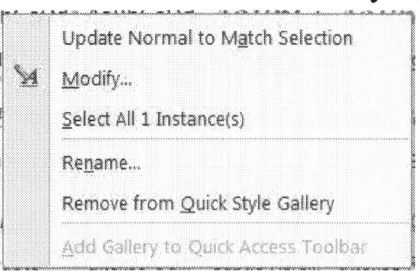

- Update Normal to Match Selection: If you already have a paragraph that is formatted correctly – Times New Roman 12, double-spaced, first line indented one-half inch, left justified, no extra space before or after – then this is a good choice. That will change your Normal style *for this document.* If any other paragraphs have the style of Normal, they will be changed, too. It is best to make style changes when you first start typing, not after you have dozens of pages that might be reformatted by a style change. "Undo" (Ctrl-z) will change your text back to what it was, but it will not undo the style change.

    If you want to make a permanent change in your "Normal" style, you need to use the next option.

- Modify. This is important, and we'll get back to it.

- Select All # Instance(s). This is how you can change everything that's Style 1 to Style 2. For example, if you want to change everything in style Subhead, and you want to change them all to Heading 3, you don't have to do it one by one. You can use this to select everything in Subhead, and then click on Heading 3; they will all be changed. But Word cannot read your mind. If you have manually modified a Normal paragraph to *look* like a subhead, Word will not recognize it as a subhead. It needs to have the right Style marker.

- You can assign a new name to the style.

- You can remove the style from the Style Gallery (what's displayed in the ribbon). That doesn't mean it's gone – just that it's harder to get to. The Gallery includes the styles that are displayed in the Styles rectangle at the top of the page. There are a lot of hidden styles that you don't normally see.

- Let's go back to "Modify." This is where you have the most control over re-defining the style. Click on this and you'll get a bigger menu:

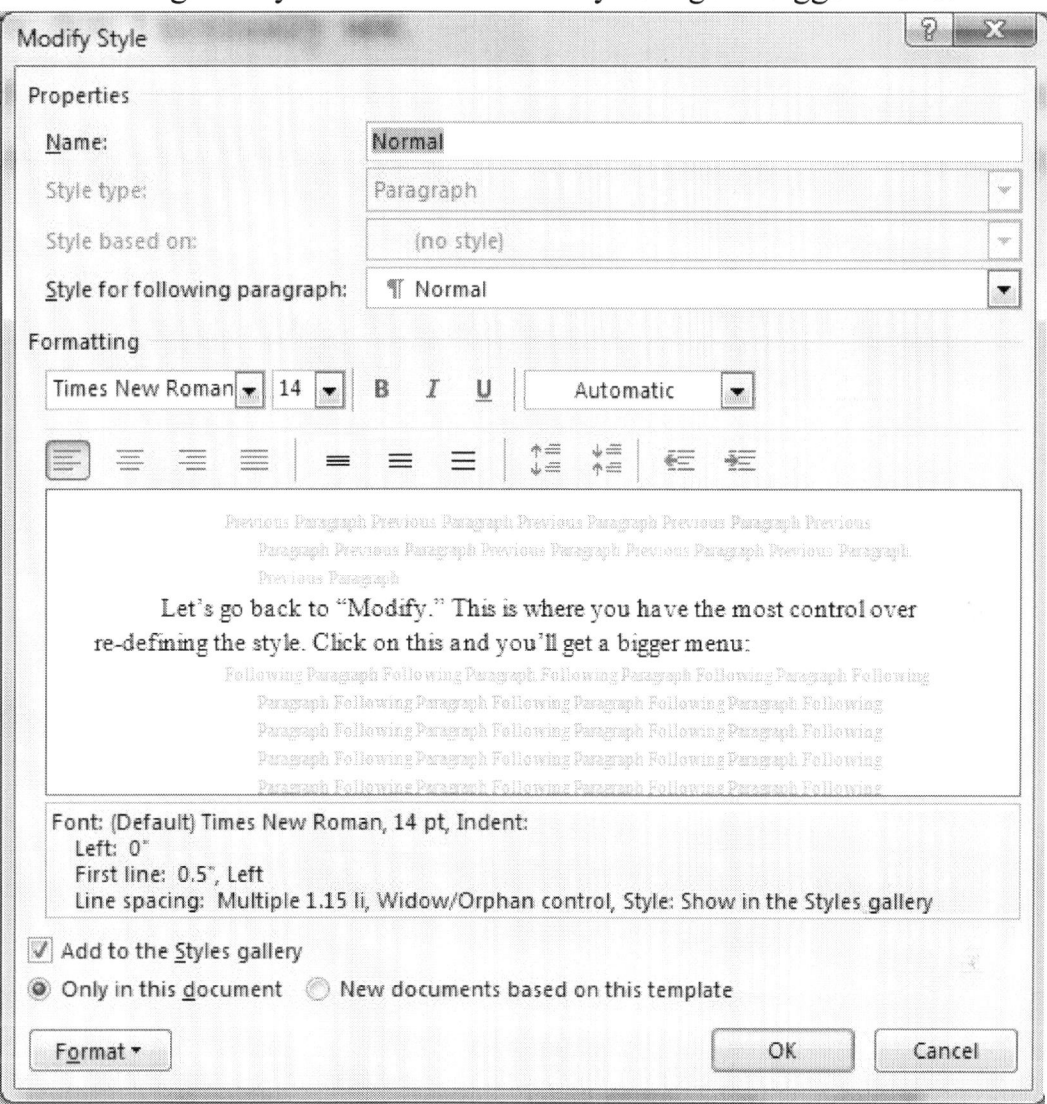

- This allows you to give a new name to the style, if you wish.
- Style for following paragraph: When you hit Enter, what style will the next paragraph be? In most cases you will want the same style, but if you have a Heading, the next paragraph is likely to be Normal rather than another Heading. You rarely need to change this.
- Formatting: For academic papers, change the font to Times New Roman, size 12. "Automatic" is the menu heading for font color. You

could change it by clicking on the triangle, but leave it at automatic, since that's usually black, except for hyperlinks.

- The menu gives you a sample of what your paragraph will look like with the settings you give it. It also displays codes. It would be nice if we could manually edit those codes in this box, but we can't.
- This Style is already in the Gallery (the styles that show in the Style box), so it is already checked.
- Next comes a very important choice: Do you want to change the style for this document only, or for all new documents based on this template? If you want a permanent change for all future documents, click here.
- You also need to change a few more *format* settings. So click on Format, and you will be asked what kind of format you want to change: font, paragraph, tabs, border, etc. You probably don't need to change anything except the paragraph format. So if you click there, you'll see the paragraph menu. Set your paragraph for:
  - o Left alignment
  - o Left indentation zero
  - o Right indentation zero
  - o Special: first line, 0.5 inch
  - o Spacing before: zero
  - o Spacing after: zero (make sure to change this)
  - o Line spacing: double
- Click OK – you have now changed the most important style.

- Heading 1 is Word's style for titles. The default is extra large, with extra space above it. Perhaps OK, but not exactly academic, either. You can change it to Times New Roman 12 (or 14), boldfaced, black.
- Heading 2 is Word's style for chapter titles.
- Heading 3 could be modified to match your subhead preferences.
- The Heading styles are very useful at a later stage, if you have a long paper. That's because Word can use them to automatically create a table of contents for you. It will keep track of your page numbers as you edit the paper. That's very useful. So if you are doing a long

paper, it can be worth your time to use the Heading styles. Another advantage of styles is that if you change your mind on (for example) how subheads should be indented or spaced, you can change them all at the same time, consistently throughout the document. Easy, once you've set it up.

Other styles to change

1. "Quote" should be modified, if you are going to use this style for academic papers. The default setting for "Quote" is to italicize the words. This is *not* a correct way to indicate quotes in academic papers. Short quotes should be put inside of quote marks (" "), and the source of the quote should be given. No special style is needed for short quotes, because they are part of normal text in a paragraph.

   Quotes longer than four or five lines, or quotes that you want to give extra attention to, should be in a separate paragraph that is indented an extra amount. The MLA style is to indent the entire paragraph one inch on the left; the Turabian stylebook says to indent a half inch on both left and right. Since the indentations show that it is a quote, quote marks are not needed. This is especially helpful if there are quote marks inside of the quote – if we have quote marks inside of quote marks, sometimes it is difficult to discern where the quotes start and stop. Having a separate paragraph for the entire quote is therefore helpful.

   So right-click on the Quote style, and modify according to the style you want to follow. For example: indent left one half inch, indent right one half inch. Some academic styles keep the paragraph double-spaced; others prefer single spacing for these block quotes. If you single space, you will need to add an extra 12 points before and after the paragraph.

2. "Book Title" is another Word style that is wrong for academic use. The default setting for this style in Word is to change the words into boldface, and to change all lower-case letters to small capitals. In academic papers, book titles should be italicized – that's all. No

boldfacing, no small caps. Italicizing the words is easier than trying to apply a style, so you may want to delete this style entirely.

3. You can define your own styles, if you wish. After you have formatted a paragraph in the way that you want, you can right-click on the paragraph, and you'll see a menu:

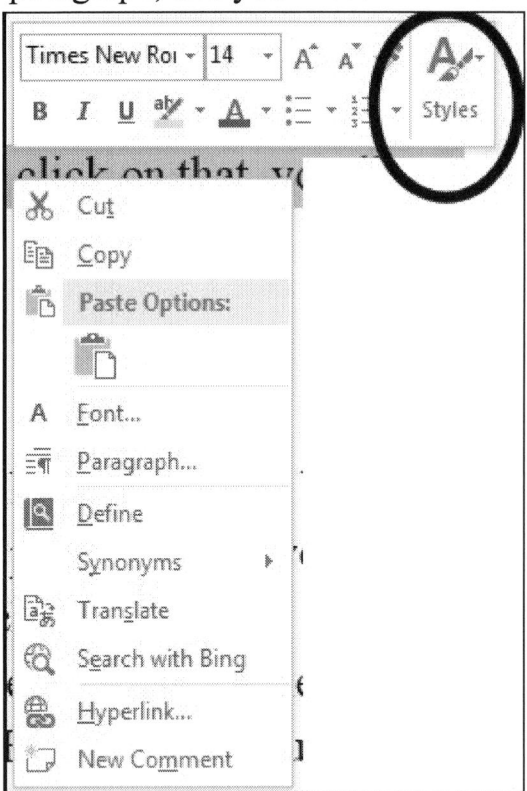

Note the last item in font menu: Styles. If you click on that, you'll get a menu of styles to choose from:

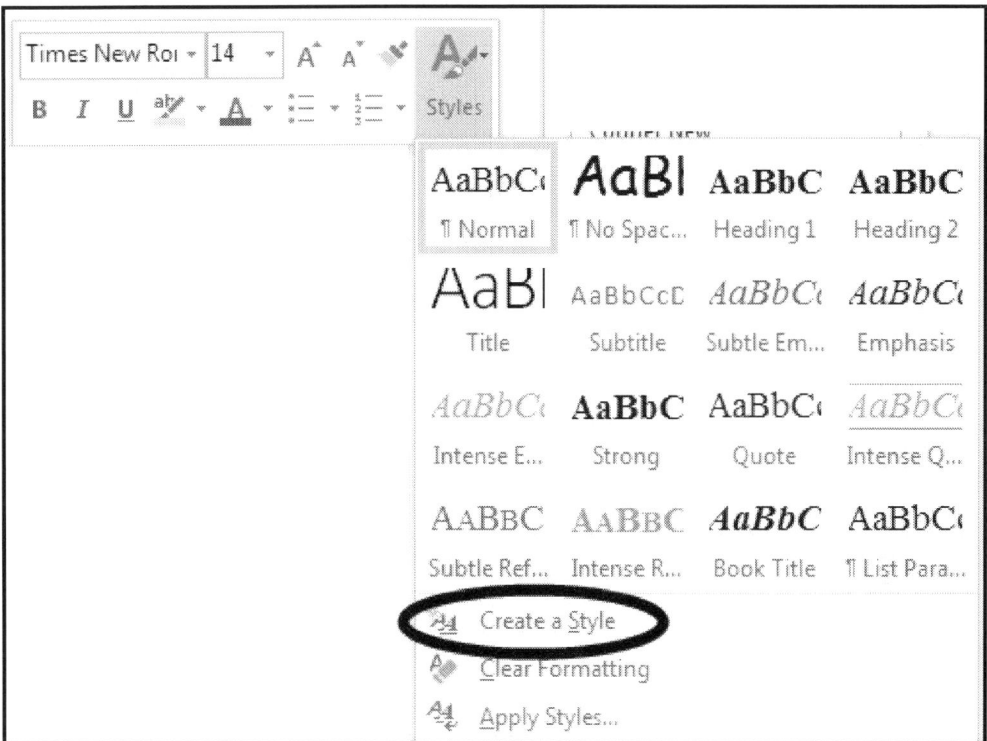

A choice near the bottom permits you to create your own style – to give it a name. You can modify it, or assign it a place in the Gallery, by modifying it – see below. Academic papers usually keep formatting simple, so you probably don't need this feature.

The Styles window

Let's look at the right-hand side of the Styles rectangle:

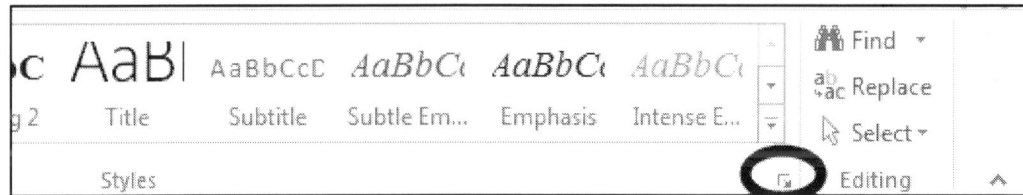

We will focus here on the small arrow at the lower-right corner. That tiny arrow leads to a huge complexity:

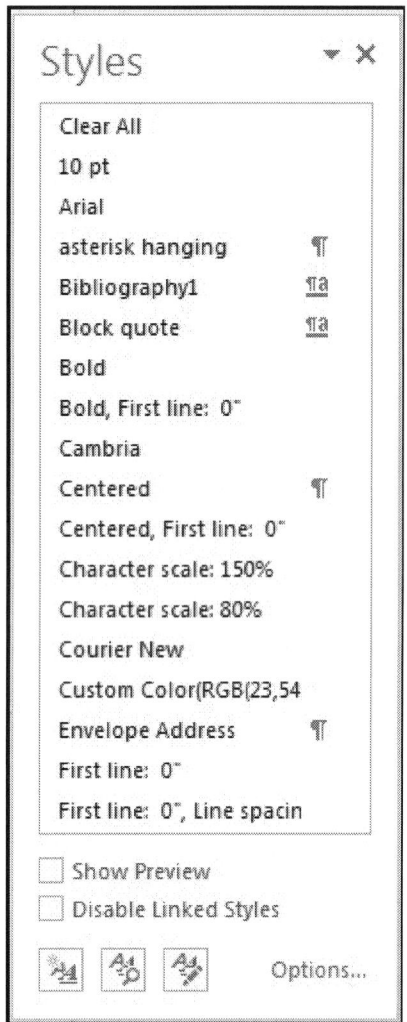

So far, this isn't very complex – it just lists the styles that are in the Gallery and in your document. The complexity comes in the lower right: "Options." If you click here, you'll get a new menu:

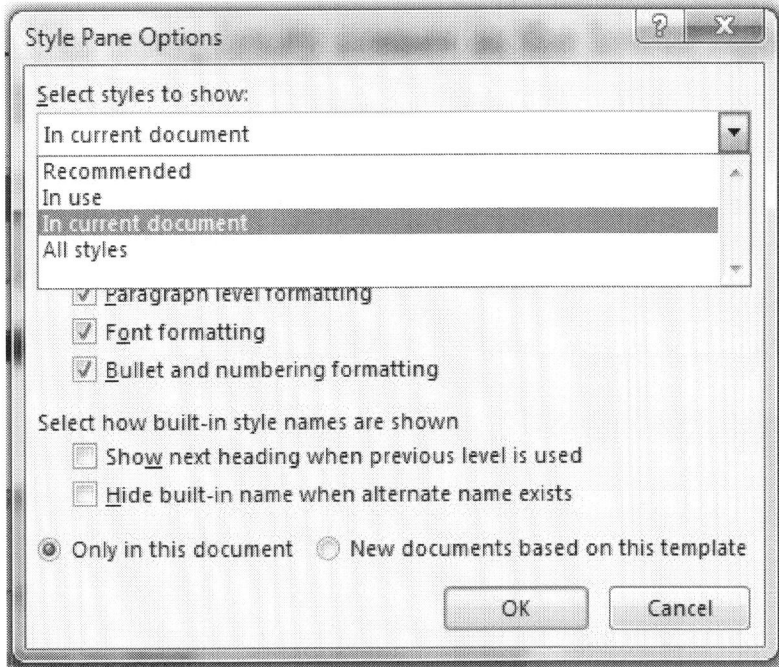

We have already clicked on the "Select Styles" to show you the dropdown options. This menu tells you that so far, you are seeing the styles that are "in current document." But if you'd like to see more, select "All styles." In the next drop-down menu, you will see that Word's default display method is to put the most recommended first:

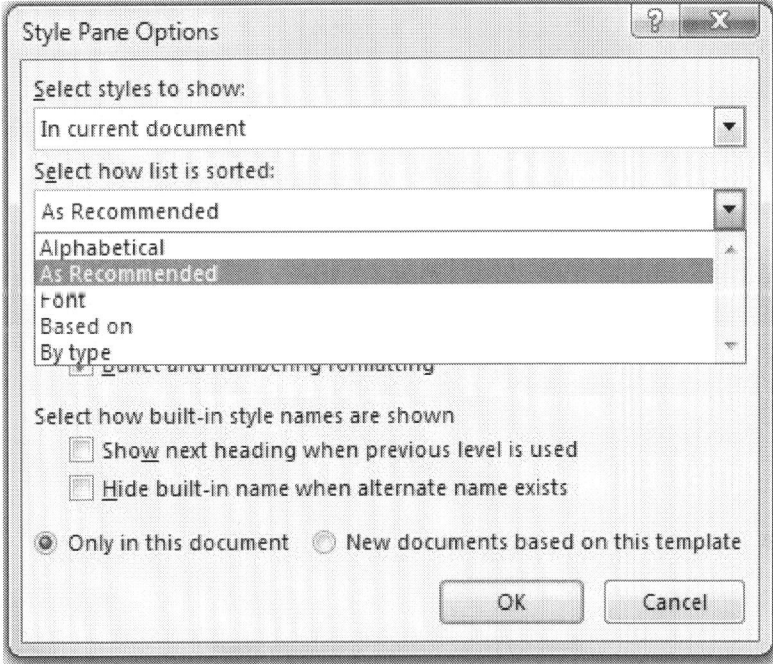

But if you want to *find* a specific style, alphabetical is the better way to list things. So click on Alphabetical, and click OK. Now the Styles window will list many more styles:

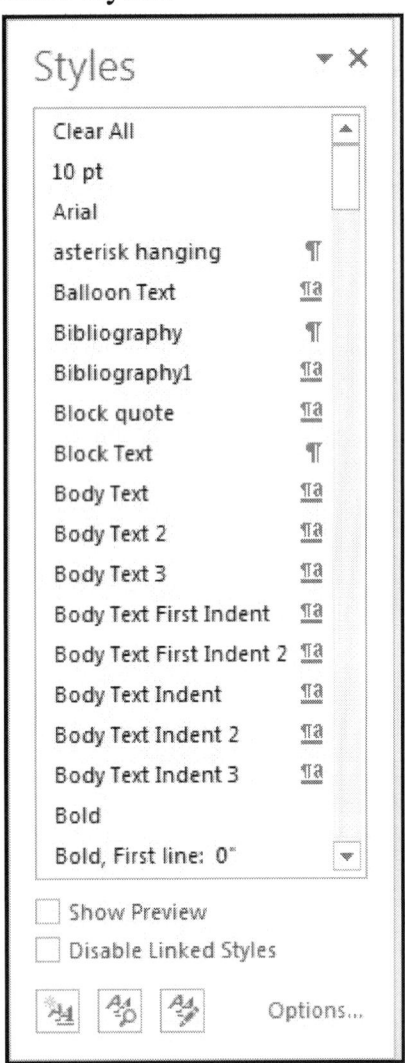

In this example, you can see only styles through the letter B. The slider in the scroll bar is only about 15 percent of the height, indicating that you are seeing only 15 percent of the styles that Word has available to it.

Note that there is a Bibliography style. Depending on which stylebook you want to follow, it may have the wrong settings for academic papers. In some stylebooks, the paragraph Special setting should be set to "Hanging," one half inch. That means the first line is at the left margin, and all subsequent lines are indented a half inch – exactly the opposite of Word's default setting.

This is the place to edit the footnote reference and footnote text styles, hyperlinks, page numbers, table of contents (TOC) entries, and balloon text for comments. (We are giving instructions *in case* you want to become more adept at using Word. But we realize all this detail isn't everyone's cup of tea.)

Editing

Over on the far right-hand side of the Home tab, just to the right of the Styles rectangle, almost out of sight, is the small Editing rectangle:

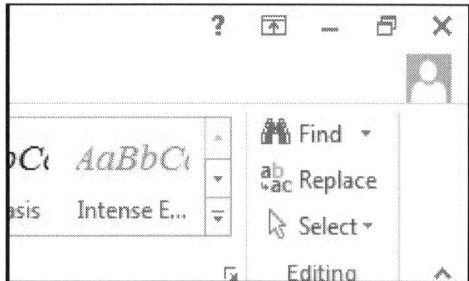

Most of this is not really about editing, and keyboard shortcuts are often easier than clicking in the ribbon.

Find (search)

If you mouse over "Find," you'll see that the keyboard shortcut is Ctrl+F. This is not correct. Ctrl+F gives you the Font menu. To get the Find menu, use the lower-case version: Ctrl+f. If you click on the small triangle to the right of Find, you will see that it offers three options: Find (which you have already seen), Advanced Find, and Go To.

- Find (Ctrl+f) works in a different way than in some older versions of Word (2007 and before), so if you are used to an older version, it may take some time to get used to the new features and options. Thankfully, most of the time a simple search does what you want. "Find" opens a Navigation pane on the left side of the document, and it will display all occurrences of whatever you type in there.

Below we have searched for the word "display":

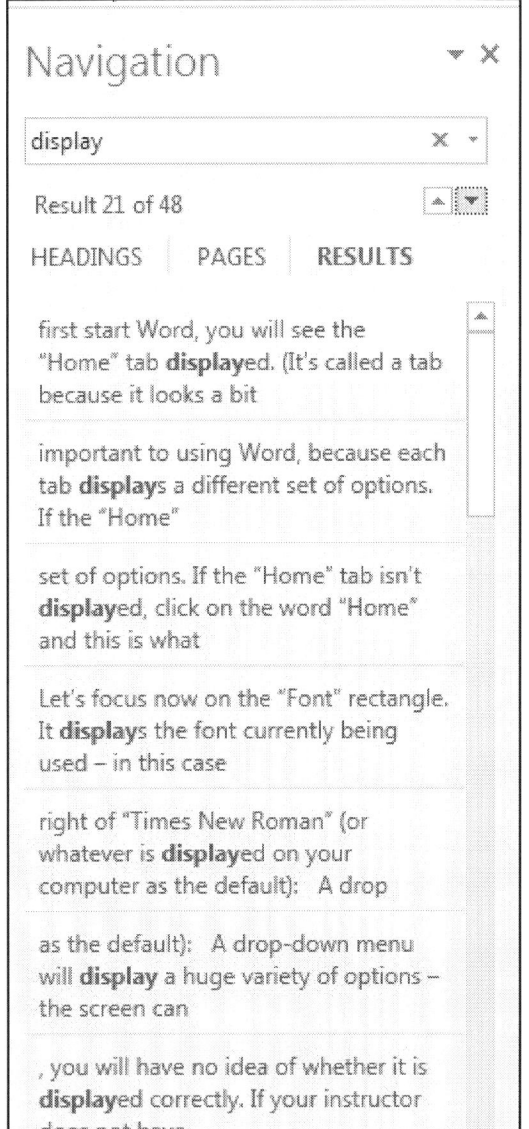

The word occurs 48 times in this document, and the next occurrence after the cursor is the 21st occurrence. In the main pane, in the center of the main window, Word displays that particular occurrence.

o The panes give the context for each occurrence. If you mouse over a pane, you will see what page it is on.

o If you click on a pane, you will be taken to that page.

o Clicking on the small triangles just below the search box will take you to the previous occurrence or the next occurrence.

- o If you hit Esc, or the small x in the search box, the search will be cleared, and you will be taken back to where you were before. The Navigation pane will remain visible.
- o Search Results is just one tab of the Navigation pane. The other two are Headings and Pages.
    - ▪ Headings displays all the paragraphs that were formatted with Styles: Heading 1, Heading 2, and Heading 3. If these Styles were not used in your document, this is not helpful.
    - ▪ Pages gives you a thumbnail picture of all your pages. This can sometimes be a good way to move around in your document.
- o If you want to move or change the size of the pane, click on the small triangle in the upper right corner of the pane.
- o If you want to get rid of the pane, click on the X in the upper right corner of the Navigation pane.
- o Now let's go back to see more options for searching. In the Navigation pane, there's a small triangle to the right of the search box:

Click on this triangle to get more options: Options, Advanced Find, Replace, Go To, and a way to search for graphics, tables, equations, or footnotes.

Here is the menu for "Options":

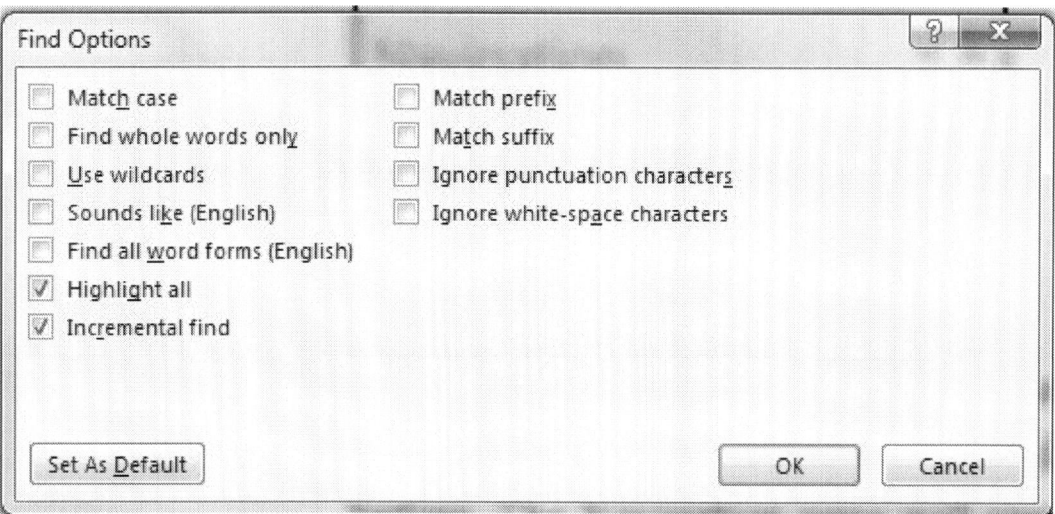

This lets you specify a case, either capitalized or lowercased, exactly as you typed it, to restrict your search, to find homonyms, etc. You can get the same options by choosing Advanced Find, and clicking on "More." It is best to avoid Wildcards for now.

o Advanced Find (Ctrl-h, Alt-d) opens a new box. This is the "Find" menu of previous versions of Word. Click on the "More" button to see the full menu:

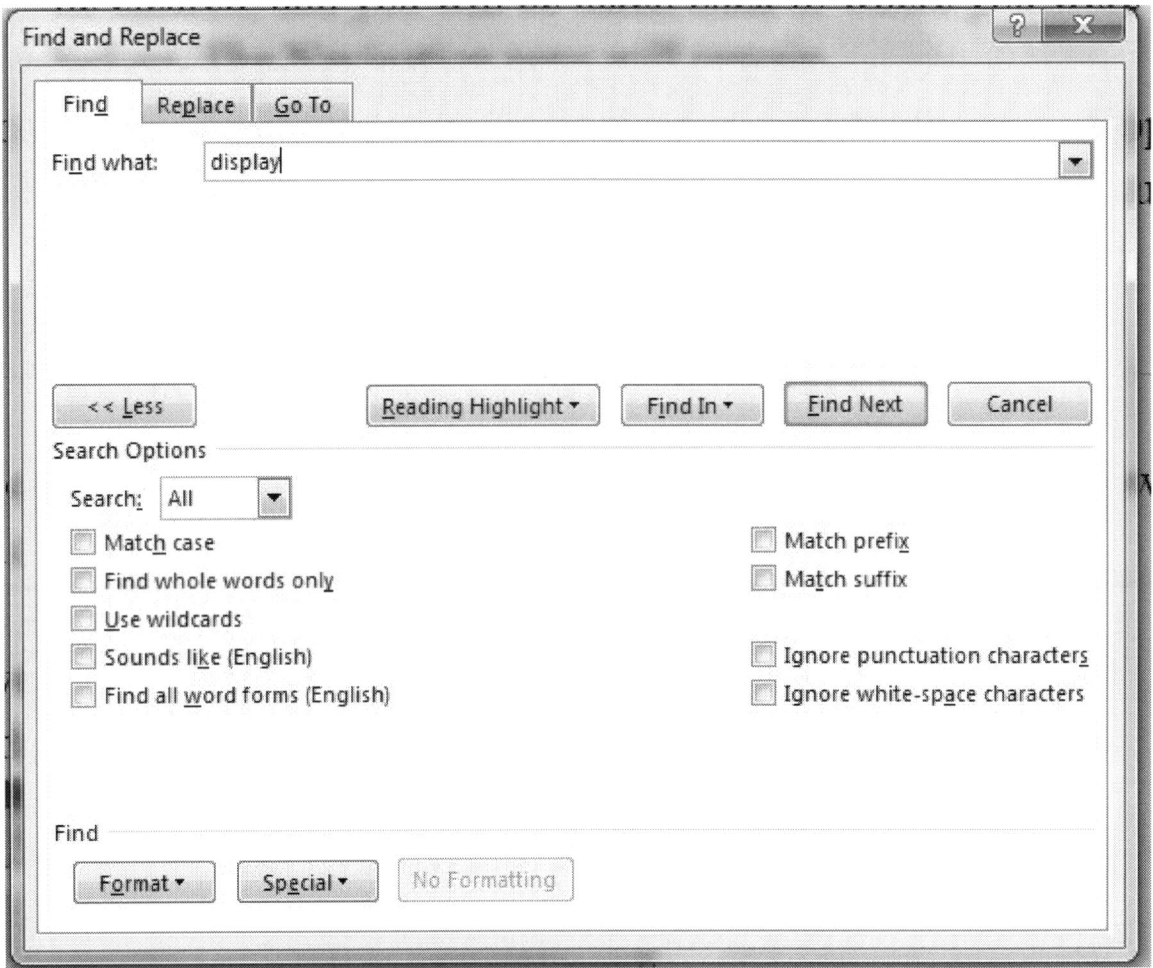

In the bottom half of the box, just after the word Search, you can choose in a drop-down menu whether to search all the document (that's the default, shown above), or only above the cursor, or only below the cursor.

The default setting for Find is to ignore case – a word will be found whether it is capitalized or not. However, occasionally it's better to specify the case, so you can. The other options are used less frequently.

In the lower left is a Format box. You can use this to search for specific format settings. The most common possibility is at the top, and as we go down the list the probability decreases even more that you will search for such things:

- You can search for a specific font, such as Calibri. Or you can search for anything that is superscripted, or bold.
- You can search for paragraph details, such as all paragraphs that are indented one half inch, or paragraphs that have line spacing 1.5.

- "Tabs" does not search for a tab character (there's a different way to do that), but it searches for tab settings – you can search for any paragraph that has a tab setting of 2.7 inches, for example.
- If you use more than one language in your document (for checking spelling, perhaps), you can search for where it may appear.
- You can also search for frames with specific characteristics, or styles, or a certain color of highlight.

When you have finished searching for a Format item, you may need to click the "No Formatting" box before your next search.

The "Special" box allows searching for a few non-keyboard characters: numbers, tab characters, dashes, line breaks, and so forth. This is the best place to use wildcards, such as search for any character, or a number. The search capabilities are large, and you can be thankful that the entire box can be made smaller by clicking the "Less" button.

In the "Reading Highlight" button, you can choose to highlight the search results, or to clear the highlighting.

With "Find In," you can restrict your search to the main text, the footnotes, or headers and footers.

Unlike most menu boxes, the Advanced Find box is a separate window, and if you switch to a different Word document, that window is still displayed. That might be useful in some cases, but at other times it's annoying. You have to exit the Advanced Find window by pressing Esc (in the upper left corner of the keyboard), or by clicking the small x in the upper right corner of the box, or by clicking on the Cancel button.

Replace

Another Find option is Replace, also known as find and replace. It is also accessible from the Home ribbon. There are two other ways to reach it:

- In the Find Navigation pane, click on the small triangle in the right of the search box, then click on Replace.
- The keyboard shortcut is easy: Ctrl-h. (Unfortunately, the letter "h" doesn't correspond with "find and replace," so it's hard to remember. Maybe all the logical letters were already being used for something else.)

The menu looks like Advanced Find (you may have noticed
that the Advanced Find box was labelled Find and Replace):

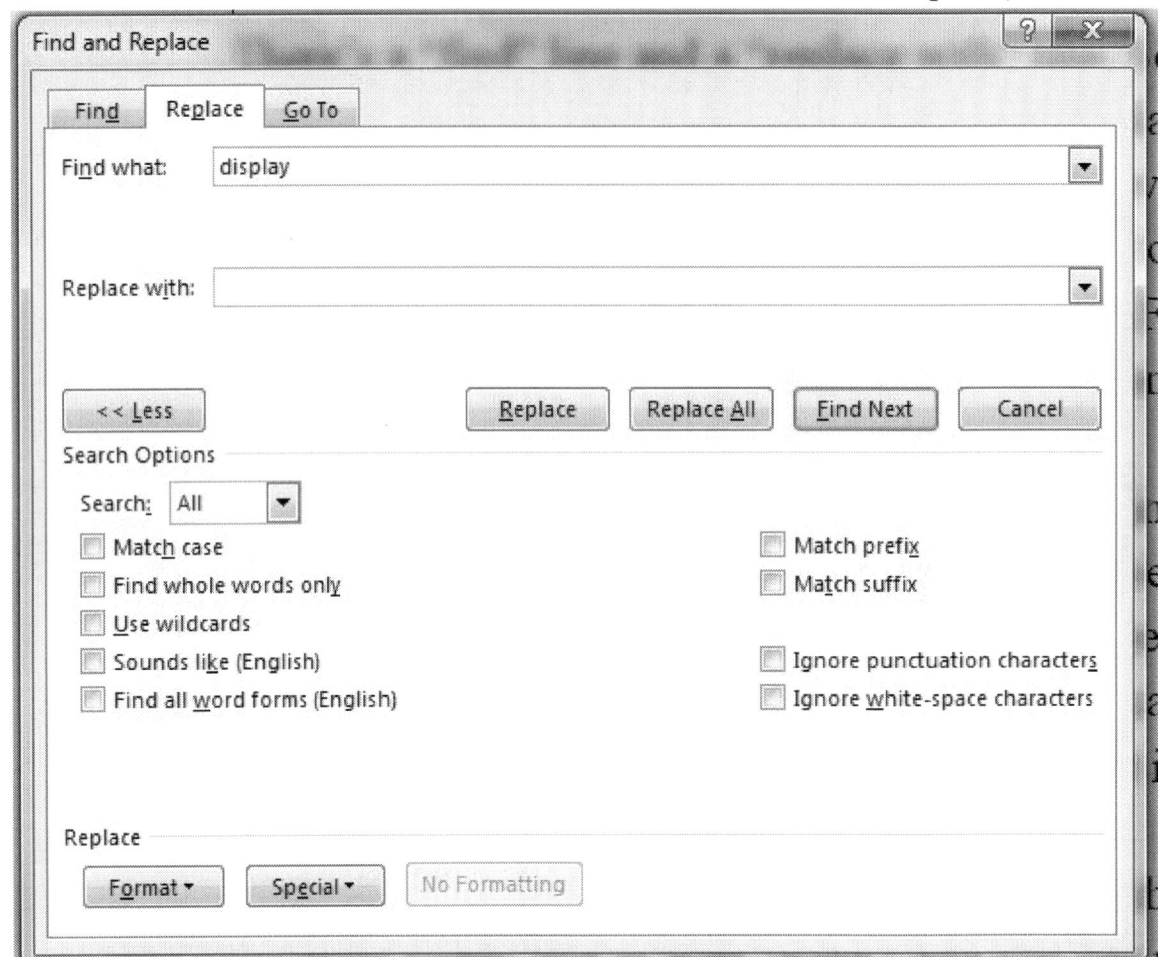

There's a "find what" line and a "replace with" line. So you can search for
every occurrence of the word "utilize," for example, and replace it with "use." If
you click on "Replace All," or press Alt-a, it will replace every occurrence, and
inform you of how many times it was done. But if you'd like to look at each
occurrence and make a decision on whether to replace it, click on Find Next (Alt-
f). Word will go to the next occurrence. If you want to replace that one, click on
Replace (Alt-r). If you don't, click on Find Next again.

Find/replace can be helpful when you are typing a paper on justification, for
example, and you'd rather not type out the word every time. When you type your
paper, you can just type "jj" instead. After you are done, you can replace every
occurrence of "jj" with "justification."

By clicking on the "more" button, you can search for additional characters
and formatting codes, just as with "Find," and you can replace them. For example,

you can automatically replace every occurrence of the word "love" and replace with the boldfaced word "**love.**" But if you have the word "glove" in your paper, part of it will be boldfaced, too. *Always be careful* with a global find and replace. If you want to delete all graphics in your document, you can search for graphics (^g) and replace them with nothing.

Go To

One of the simplest functions is Go To (Ctrl-g).

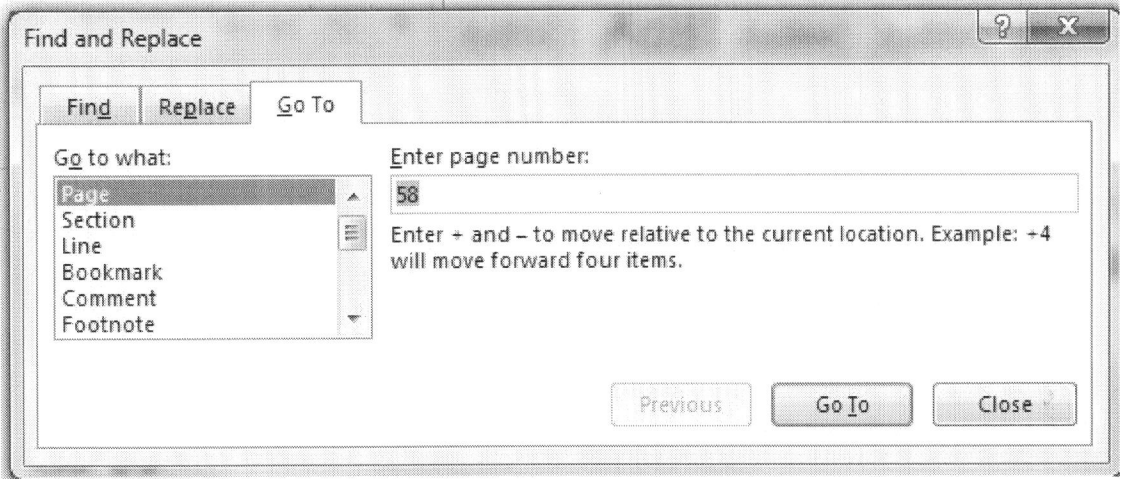

Just type in the page number you want, and press Enter, or click on Next, and Word zips to the top of the page you requested. This can be a bit tricky if you start renumbering pages somewhere in your paper, but most people don't do that. Hit Esc to get rid of the window.

Wait – there's more! Notice the menu at the left: you can also go to a specific section, line, bookmark, comment (if you have set any up), or a footnote (that can be useful), endnote, etc. Also notice the small print on the right side – there is a way to go forward or backward a specific number of pages.

Select

The Select menu is not very useful. The first choice is to Select All – your entire document (keyboard shortcut Ctrl-a).

The second choice is to Select Objects, but most academic papers don't have any.

The third choice is to select text with similar formatting, which means the same paragraph style. This might include your entire paper, too.

Last, you can display the Selection pane, which is not very useful, either.

Undo

Perhaps the most important editing function is not even in the editing box. It is Undo – to go backwards in your editing or typing history. If you have goofed, you need a way to reverse what you've done. The keyboard shortcut Ctrl-z. The icon for this is in the Quick Access toolbar, in the extreme upper left of your window, no matter what ribbon is displayed:

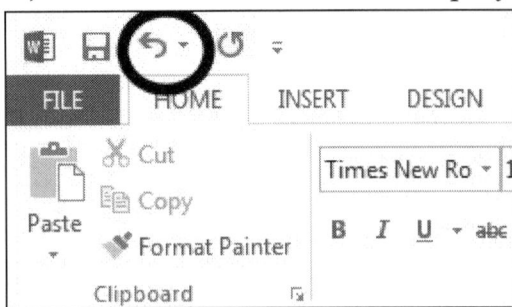

You can hit Ctrl-z or click the icon numerous times to back up numerous steps, all the way back to your most recent save. If you click on the small triangle, you'll see a list of what has been done – you can zip to earlier edits if you want.

If you have gone back too far, Ctrl-y will take you forward one step at a time. Or click on the Quick Access icon just to the right of Undo.

You can customize the Quick Access toolbar and put additional icons into it. If you use certain commands frequently, this will make them more accessible, since the Quick Access toolbar is always displayed no matter which ribbon is visible. To customize, click (on the right end of the Quick Access toolbar) the icon of a line over a triangle.

Insert

The Insert tab includes several functions that are of minimal value for academic papers, but a few can be very helpful. We'll look at them from left to right.

1. Cover page: Word supplies several templates for cover pages for various reports. Most academic papers *do not need* fancy cover pages. Include one only if you are requested to do so. Shorter class papers usually have the "cover page" info in the upper left corner: Student's name, the instructor's name, course name, and date. The fifth line is the title, centered. The paper itself begins on line six.
2. "Blank page" inserts a blank page (one or two page breaks). Academic papers do not need blank pages. You might want one if you always want a chapter to begin on an odd-numbered page, but the best way to do that is to go to the Page Layout ribbon, choose Breaks, then Odd Page. Or Alt-p, b, d. Then Word will figure out whether you need a blank page.
3. "Page break" inserts a page break. It can be used in front of the Works Cited section.

Working with tables

Academic papers occasionally need a table. The options are enormous; we'll give only a brief introduction. After you click on the "Table" box, you'll see a grid, and you can move your mouse over it to highlight certain cells:

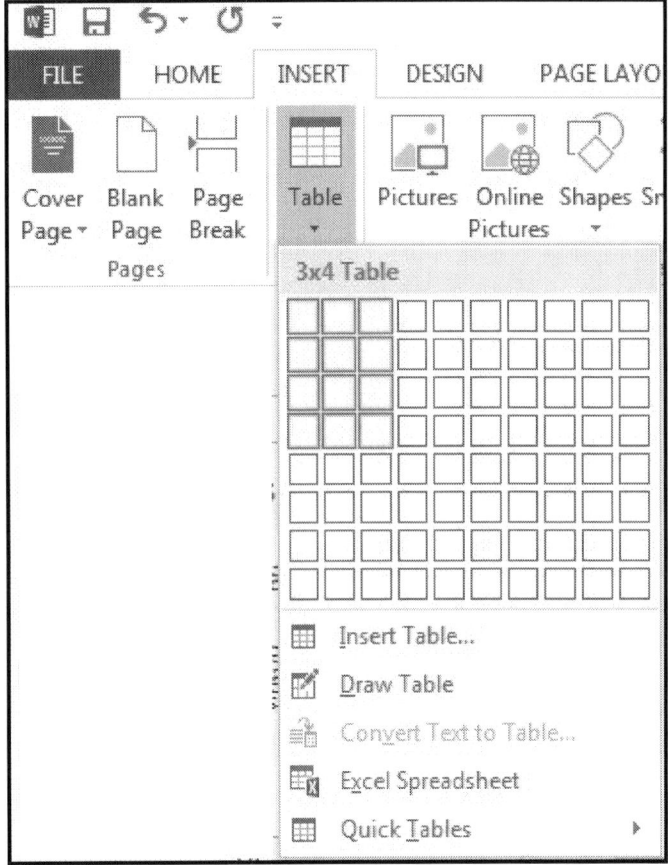

a. As you move the mouse across the table, a different number of squares will be highlighted. Our illustration shows a table three columns wide and four rows high. Word will also display in your document what the table will look like when spread across your page. This is just a temporary display – it's not implemented until you click in the grid. And it can be modified after that.

b. "Insert Table" gives you a different menu. It does some of the same things – only here you are working with numbers rather than a visual grid:

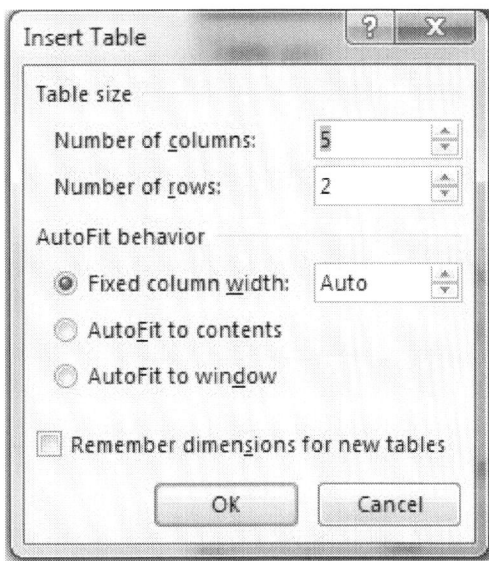

i. Type in the number of columns and rows you want.

ii. Choose a column width. "Auto" spreads equal-width columns across to the right-hand margin. Otherwise, you can specify in inches how wide you want all the columns to be. (You can always adjust it later.)

iii. "AutoFit to contents" will make the columns vary in width according to the content. If there's a lot of text in column 3, for example, Word will make column 3 wider (even as you type). This is probably best for most tables.

iv. If you check the last box, Word will remember the kind of table you prefer; this is useful if you are going to make several similar tables.

c. "Draw table" gives you a lot of flexibility: it transforms the mouse into a pencil icon. Start in one corner and drag your pencil to the other corner. Word will create a rectangle for you – the outer boundaries of your new table. After that, you can draw in new lines to create columns and rows – even partial rows and split cells. You can even have a diagonal:

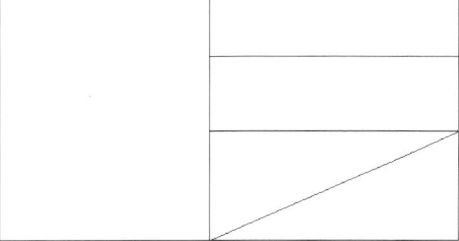

d. "Convert text to table" will (if you highlighted some text before you clicked on "Insert Table") transform that text into a table, separating the columns according to where you put tab spaces, commas, or whatever character you specify.

e. "Excel Spreadsheet" inserts a spreadsheet – and that's too complicated for this tutorial! Not needed in most academic papers, unless you are in economics.

f. "Quick tables" shows a small variety of table templates.

How do you modify a table?

After you have created a table, how can you modify it? Click anywhere inside the table, and Word will add more options to the tabs it displays in the menu ribbon at the top of the page. Tables have so many options that *two* ribbons are needed. We show first the table Design ribbon, then the table Layout ribbon:

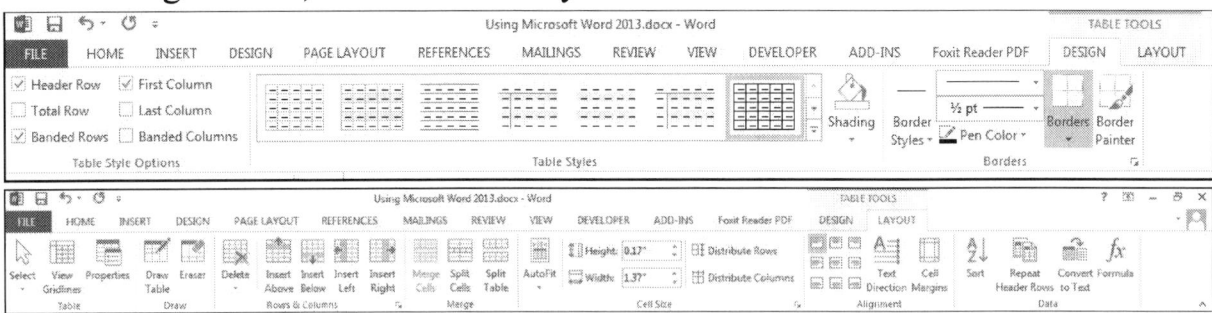

A table header row generally has labels for the column. If the table has so many rows that it has to extend to a second page, the header row can be automatically repeated.

Table styles are complicated, like paragraph styles. All sorts of colors, borders, and shading schemes can be used, or new styles created.

The layout ribbon is most useful – this is how you can (from left to right) delete rows or columns, add rows or columns, merge or split cells, specify exact row heights or column widths, force the columns or rows to be of equal width, align text inside of the cells, sort the data in the table, or convert the entire table into ordinary text.

We won't attempt to walk you through all the possibilities, but we'll just let you know that these possibilities exist, and if you want one of them, then you can experiment to see how it's done. Or go to one of the tutorials on the Microsoft site, other user sites, or YouTube.

With "formula," you can perform some mathematical functions. Adding up a column is easy (that's the default function); all the others are more complicated.

And with that extremely abbreviated discussion of tables, we will resume our survey of the "Insert" tab.

Working with pictures

Some academic papers include pictures, and this is one starting point for working with images. There are two ways to insert a picture:

1. In a graphics program, such as Paint.NET, select the picture you want, or select a portion of a picture, and copy it (Ctrl-c). Then go to Word, put your cursor in the location you want, and paste the picture (Ctrl-v, or Shift-Insert, or click Paste in the Home ribbon).
2. On the Insert tab, click on Pictures, and a new window will pop up, similar to Windows Explorer (Alt-n, p gives you the same window). In this window, you can navigate in your own computer to find the picture you want to insert. (If you don't know where you stored that picture, the window also includes a search feature. If you don't remember the picture's name, you are out of luck.)

Once you have the picture, you can adjust it. There are at least two ways to do this.

1. If you right-click on the picture, you'll get a menu. If you choose Format Picture, that will open up a new pane on the right called Format Picture.

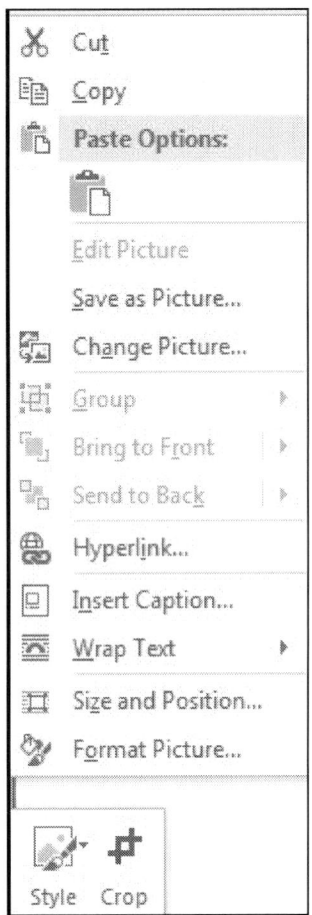

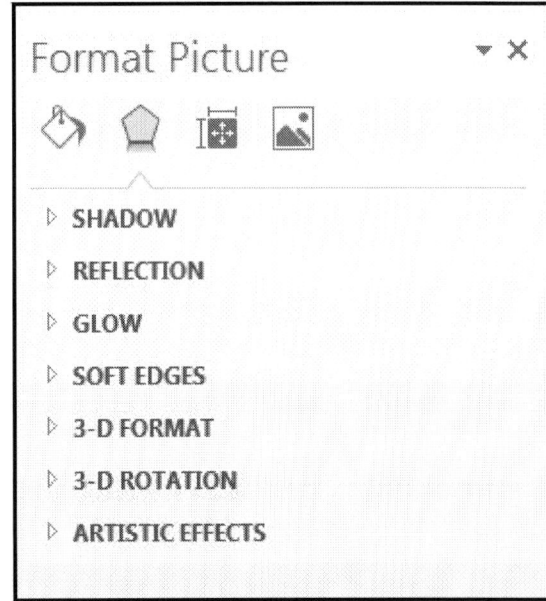

The Format Picture pane has several options. Most functions are easier to use in the second method: Word's menu at the top of the page.

2. If you click on a picture, the menu ribbon at the top of Word will display a new option: Picture Tools. Click on the word "Format" to see the options:

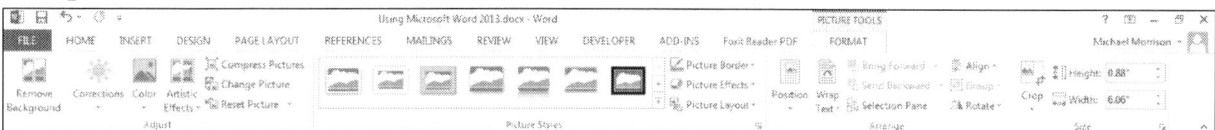

You can adjust the image brightness, contrast, and color. You can compress it so that it takes up less disk space – a feature that becomes more important as the number of megapixels in cameras keeps rising.

You can give the entire picture a "shadow" on two sides, and give it a border of various colors and weights.

With "Position," you can force it to a certain location on the page, or let it move when its associated text moves. Picture location can be frustrating. If you tell Word that you want the picture in the upper right corner, it might sometimes jump to the upper right corner of the *next* page; it depends on where the picture was originally inserted into the text. So it is best not to worry too much about picture locations until you are almost done with your document. Then position them, starting from page 1 working down toward the end. That way an edit on one picture won't change the location of a later picture.

When you click on a picture, a small Layout Options icon appears to the upper right of the picture. This lets you set whether text overlaps your picture (or your picture covers up part of the text!), and how much distance there is between text and picture.

This has been a very brief overview of what Word can do with images. We kept it simple because *you* need to keep it simple for most academic papers. This is not an art project (unless the instructor requests that it be).

For that reason, academic papers should rarely use the next few icons in the Insert menu: Online Pictures, Shapes, SmartArt, Charts (the latter might be good for some business papers – but they are complicated!), or a Screenshot of another program that's running on your computer.

Links

In the center of the Insert ribbon, Word gives you three types of links:

1. First, the hyperlink that you are probably familiar with from the Internet. In Word, if you type an internet address starting with www, such as www.google.com and follow it with a space, the default for Word is to automatically turn that address into an active hyperlink: blue text, and underlined. That's not exactly standard for academic papers, but since Word does this by default, most instructors are used to it. If you don't want this, there are four ways to change it:

    a. You can highlight the text, and manually turn it back into black, and remove the underline.

    b. You can right-click on the text, and choose "Remove hyperlink."

    c. If you want a more permanent change, you can position your cursor over the first w, and a faint double blue underline will appear. Move your mouse over the blue underline, and a tiny menu will appear. Click on the triangle, and one of the options will be "Stop Automatically Creating Hyperlinks." This is part of Word's AutoCorrect feature that can be customized.

    d. You can edit Word's style for "Hyperlink" and "Followed Hyperlink." You will have to list all styles, and modify those two. See our section on Styles to see how to do it. The text will still be a hyperlink, but not be blue or underlined.

    If you have an internet address that does not start with www, such as news.google.com, Word does not automatically turn it into a hyperlink. But if you *want* it to be an active hyperlink, you can highlight the words, click Hyperlink, and type in the correct address. Be sure to begin the address with http:// (otherwise it will look for that address in your own computer). You can save yourself the extra steps by including http:// as part of the web address in the main text, and Word will automatically turn it into an active link. For example, http://news.google.com.

2. "Bookmark" is like an internal hyperlink. You can highlight text, such as a subhead, and then click Bookmark. Give it a name (must start with a letter, no spaces allowed), then click Add. Then, from anywhere else in the document, you can create a link to that bookmark. (This is not necessary if you use the Style "Heading 3" for your subheads, since "cross-reference" allows you to link to any of the heading Styles.)

3. "Cross-reference" allows you to create a link to any heading, bookmark, footnote, or any paragraph that is part of a numbered list. You can link to the page number, the full paragraph text, etc. After you make edits, even re-arrange the text, Word can re-calculate all the page numbers so the cross references are correct. This is very useful if you are creating a manual with a lot of cross references, but it's probably not needed in an academic paper.

Headers and Footers

A "header" is text that automatically appears within the top margin of every pages; a "footer" is text that automatically appears within the bottom margin. This can be words such as "John Smith, Sociology Assignment 3, Feb. 13, 2013, page x." A simpler format is "Smith x," where "x" is the page number. In MLA format, this should be a right-justified header. In some academic papers, it can be a footer. Unfortunately, this is not one of Word's sample templates.

Click on Header (or Footer, if that's what you want), and you'll get options:

Click on the first option, labeled "Blank." That will take you to the header, where you can type in the text that you want, such as your name. (Note that the header text is now in black; the main text of your paper is gray. This shows you what part of the page is active.) Press Ctrl-r to move the text to the right margin, then press End so that your cursor goes to the end of the line. Press the space bar once to create a space. In the Insert Ribbon, click on Page Number, then Current Position, then Plain. Automatic numbering is a great feature! You are done, so either click on "Close Header" in the Insert ribbon, or else double-click anywhere in your main text.

Word now displays the main text in black, and the header (and footer) in gray. (This is in the Print Layout view, so you can see what the page will look like when printed.)

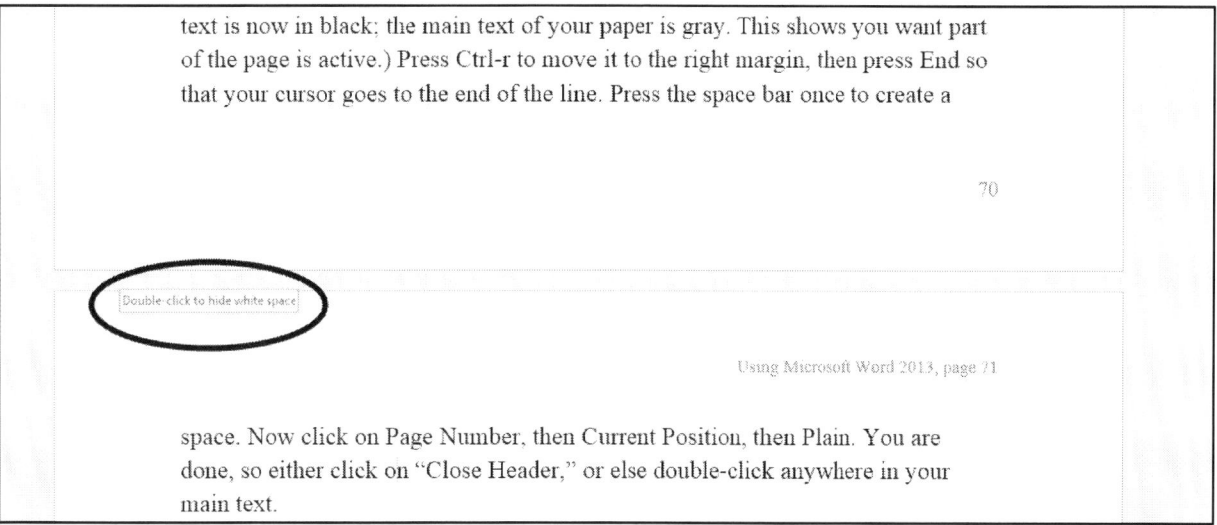

A lot of white space is displayed. This can cause sudden jumps when you are scrolling your cursor down the pages. To hide this white space, double-click in the crack between the pages, as circled above. If you double-click in the header area, however (and it's not far away), Word will think you want to edit the header, and activate it – so aim carefully.

Page number: If all you want is to insert an automatic page number in the top or bottom margins, without any additional text, then you can click on Page Number from the Insert tab menu.

Text boxes, Quick Parts, WordArt, drop cap, and symbols

The last few icons in the Insert menu are:

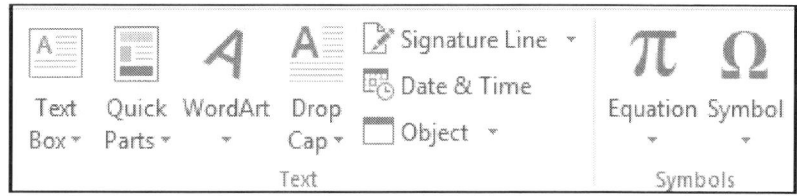

Text box is a useful feature for projects and business reports. It's good for putting extra information into a box, or to highlight an important quote from the main text. Word supplies a few formats to choose from.

Quick Parts are not quick – at least not quick to learn. With "Field," you can get Word to automatically put certain kinds of data into your document, such as the date, the number of pages, the document name, the year, and many other types of information. "Building blocks" gives you options on text boxes, cover page templates, equations, footers, etc. For many of these possibilities, there are other ways to access the same feature.

WordArt can give you fancy effects for titles and captions. It can also make your research paper look like a comic book. Not a good idea.

Drop Cap makes the first character in your paragraph extra large. This can be an artistic effect in newsletters and magazine articles.

Signature Line is a digital signature service provided by Microsoft.

Date & Time can insert the exact time that you print the document.

Object can insert items from other programs.

Equation is useful for mathematics.

Symbol is useful for characters that aren't on the keyboard, including accent marks, Greek, Hebrew, and other alphabets, and odd characters such as ¡ ¢ £ ¥ § © « ® ± ¾ ₴ and many others. If you submit your papers electronically, your foreign-language characters may not display correctly on your instructor's computer if they are in a font set the instructor does not have. But if you use the Insert Symbol feature, they are more likely to display and print correctly.

Spelling Check and Review Tab

Some parts of the Review tab ribbon are very important for academic papers. The most important functions are on the left, in the "Proofing" rectangle:

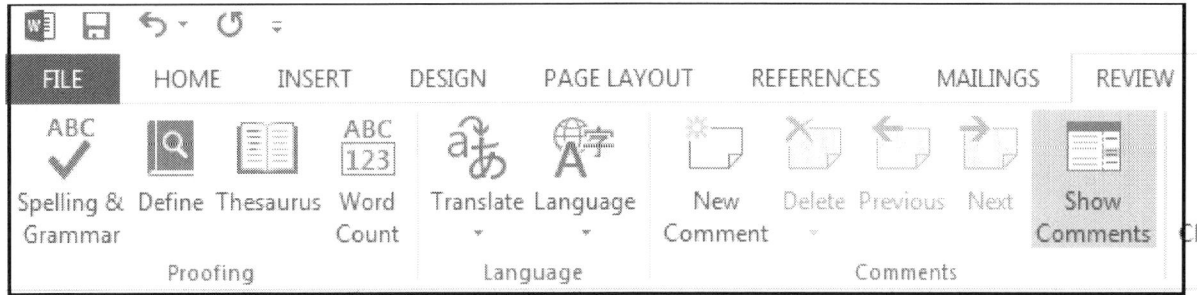

Spelling & Grammar is one of the most useful functions of any word processing program. This can save you a multitude of errors – but it does not completely do away with the need for proofreading, either. A computer will think that "not" is just as good as "now," even though the meanings are opposite. "Then" and "than" and "that" may be equally acceptable to the program, but not to your instructor.

Spell-checkers don't always identify problems with apostrophes. Word thinks that "Jesus disciples" is just as good as "Jesus' disciples," although only the latter one is correct. "It's" with an apostrophe always means "it is"; "its" without an apostrophe means "belonging to it." The word-processing program can help you with some things, but you still need to know the rules of spelling and grammar yourself.

The built-in dictionaries are good, but not perfect – they don't have all the words in specialized academic fields, so you will need to teach the program a few things. Suppose you are writing a paper about Ahaziah – you will notice that Word automatically puts a squiggly red line under the word: Ahaziah . The red squiggle will not print – it just means that the word is not in the program's dictionary. For many words, it means that you didn't spell it right. But in this case you have a perfectly legitimate word that isn't in Word's default dictionary.

Some people don't like seeing those red squiggles, so they turn them off. That is a bad idea. It is like disabling your gas gauge because you don't want to know that your car is low on gas. So keep those red squiggles turned on, and do something about them. If the word is spelled wrong, fix it. If it's spelled correctly, let Word know that it's OK.

If you right-click on the red squiggle, you'll get a small menu:

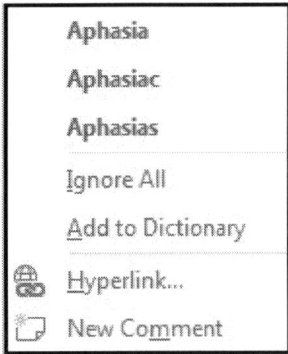

a. At the top, Word has given you a few similar words that *are* in its dictionary, but in this case they are just as obscure as Ahaziah is. But if you were really trying to type Aphasia, then Word is giving you an easy way to correct your spelling – just click on the spelling you want.

b. If you want Word to ignore all occurrences *in this document,* then click on "Ignore All."

c. If you want Word to accept Ahaziah from now on, in all documents, click on "Add to Dictionary."

What happens if you see in your document a wrongly spelled word, such as quat, and it doesn't have a red squiggle underneath it? There are several possible explanations.

      a. You have accidentally told Word to accept "quat" as a legitimate word. Now you need to edit the dictionary. In the upper left corner, click on the File tab (or press Alt-f), then click on Options, then Proofing, then Custom Dictionaries, then Edit Word List.

      b. You (or whoever created the document in the first place) has checked the spelling in the document, and told Word to ignore this word. And it remembers. There are two ways to fix this:

            1. To clear its memory, you need to highlight the word, paragraph, or the entire document (Alt-a), and then in the Review tab, click on Set Language. Make sure the correct language is checked (quat is a legitimate word in some languages), and check the box that says "Do not check spelling or grammar." Of course this is

precisely what you *do* want to do, so you will have to go back and repeat the process: click on Set Language, and then uncheck the box that says "Do not check spelling or grammar."

2. Click in the Office Button (the circle in the upper left corner) (or press Alt-f), then click on Word Options, then Proofing, then Recheck Document.

AutoCorrect

Word will fix many of your problems while you type. The AutoCorrect feature will automatically turn "teh" into "the." And it will fix incorrect spellings of believe, travelling, protégé, and a large number of other words, including "misspelled." This is a *very* useful feature.

But occasionally AutoCorrect will make mistakes, and if you want to write about the literary device of inclusio, you will have to tell Word to stop changing that word into something else. The moral of the story again is that Word can help you, but you still need to do your own proofreading, too.

You can create new AutoCorrect combinations, if you want to. But Word does not make this very easy to get to. Here are two ways:

1. To adjust the options, you can click on the "File" tab in the upper left (or press Alt-f), then click on Options, then Proofing, then AutoCorrect Options.

2. Spell a word incorrectly. For example, type teh, and Word will automatically change it to "the." If you hold the mouse over the first

letter, a blue double line will appear under the first letter:

a. If you move the mouse down slightly and hold it over the blue double line, you can see a triangle link to a new menu. Click on the little triangle to see your options:

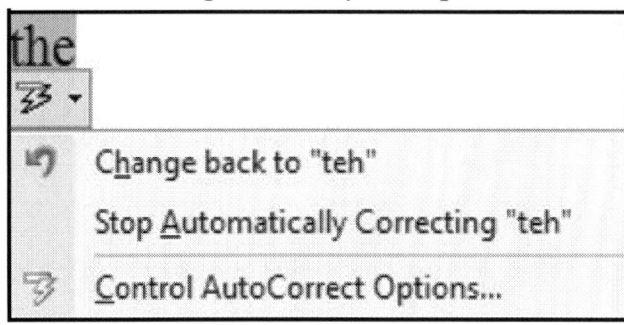

b. If you click on Control AutoCorrect Options (or if you press the c key – note that the letter C is the underlined), you will see a menu:

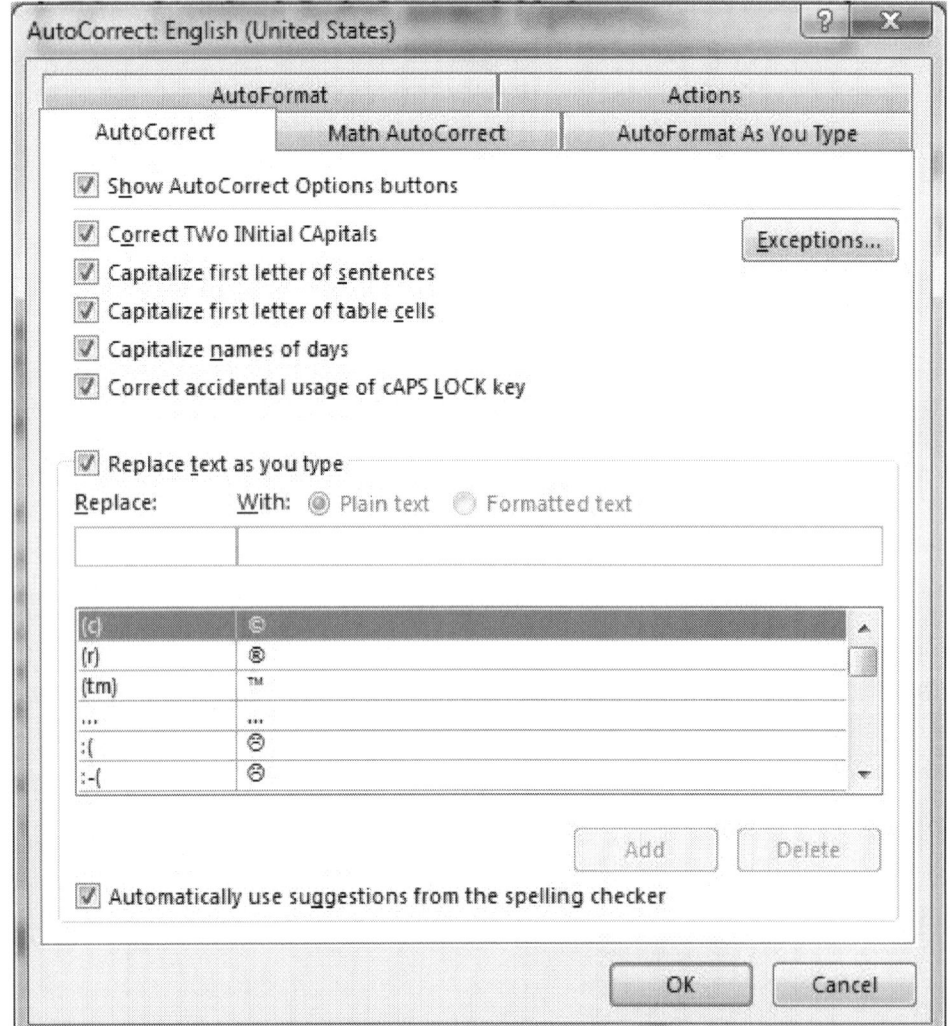

Each of the five tabs at top will show you options for different categories of AutoCorrect. We'll just note one on the AutoCorrect tab. You can type something into the "Replace" box, and then something into the "With" box. For example, suppose you type the word "Higginbotham" frequently and would like to save some keystrokes. You could tell Word to automatically replace "hh" with "Higginbotham."

Checking spelling and grammar for the entire document

So far we have discussed spelling corrections word by word. But it is helpful, once you have done all your research and all your typing, to check the entire document one more time. This is when you click on (at last we get to an icon on the Review ribbon!) "Spelling & Grammar." Or you can press F7 – that also starts the spelling and grammar check. Either way, Word begins at where your cursor is, and displays the first problem it finds in the pane on the right. There, it will present you a menu of options of what to do with this word. For example:

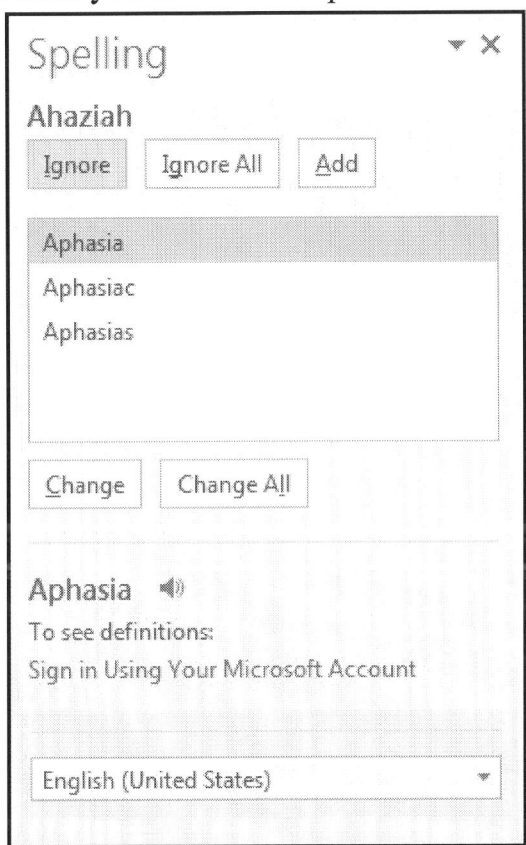

You can choose to ignore the word this one time, ignore all occurrences in this document, or add it to the dictionary in order to ignore it in all future documents, too.

In the bottom half of the menu, Word displays some similar words that *are* in its dictionary. You can even hear what the words pronounced. If one of those words is correct, you can click on it. Then you can choose to change this one occurrence, or change all occurrences in this document.

Once you have done that, Word will resume scanning your document for possible problems.

Word will also check your grammar and writing style. Word puts a red squiggly line under spelling problems, and a blue squiggly line underneath stylistic problems.

It overlooks many grammar problems, and flags too many stylistic errors. For example, it sees nothing wrong with "We was doing that." However, it will object to every use of the passive voice, and every contraction. In my opinion, a program that sees nothing wrong with "we was" has no right to complain about stylistic questions that are more debatable. If your instructor is fussy about passive voice and contractions, then Word can be helpful. But if you'd rather turn this feature off, click on the File tab, then Options, then Proofing, then Settings. Uncheck contractions and passive sentences.

One option for the spelling & grammar check is to show readability statistics. It works only if you check grammar. Here's the report for this document:

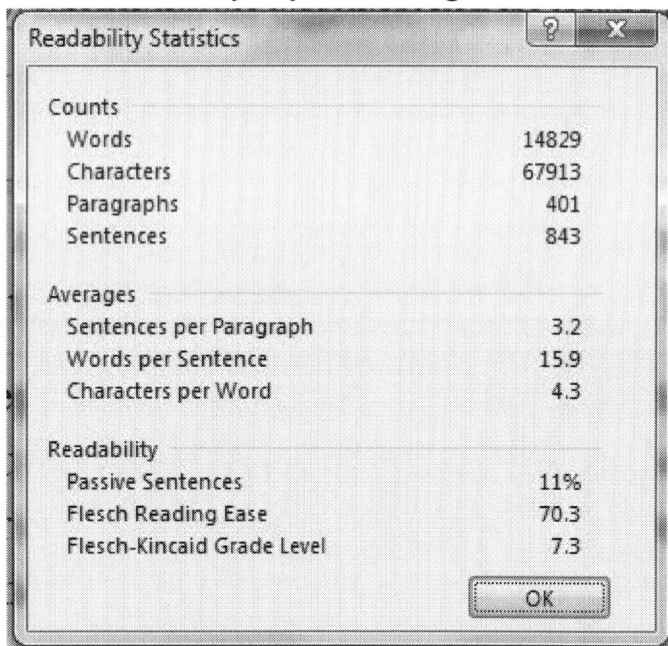

This tells you the number of words, characters, paragraphs, and sentences in your document. It gives you some additional statistics, and estimates that you need to be in seventh grade in order to understand this document. (That is based on the grammar, not the technology!)

Research, thesaurus, translate, and word count

Let's resume our overview of the Review tab menu ribbon.

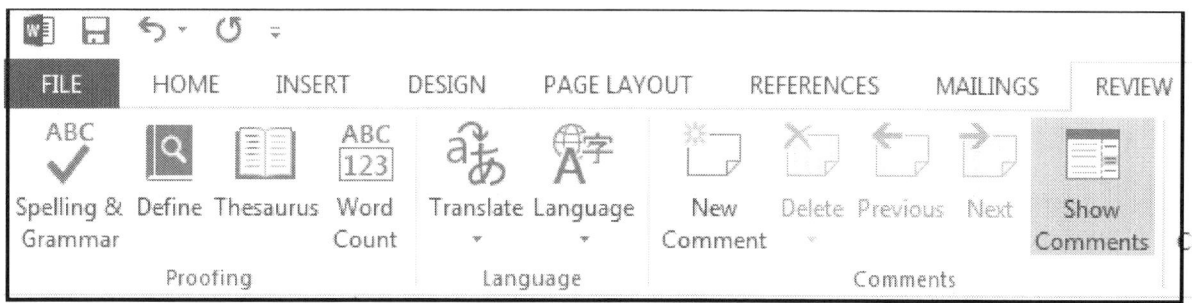

"Define" will look words up in a dictionary, if you are signed in to a Microsoft account.

"Thesaurus" (or Shift-F7) can give you words that have similar meaning. But don't pick words you are not familiar with – you may end up picking words that have connotations that aren't appropriate.

"Word count" sounds useless, because the document's word count is always displayed in the lower left corner of your screen. But the "Word Count" icon gives you some additional statistics:

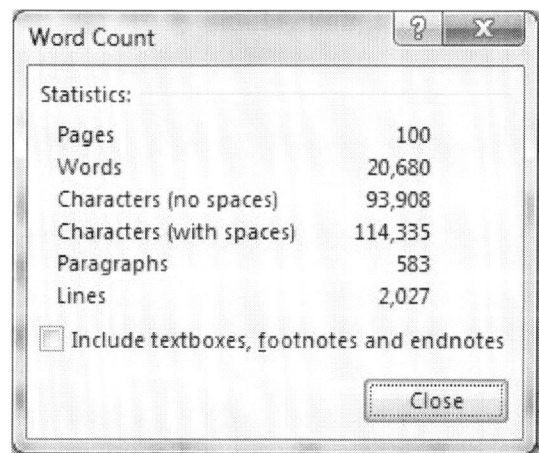

"Translate" can give you rudimentary translations into a few other languages. But don't trust it very far – Word does not know their rules of grammar any better than it does English grammar, and it does not know figures of speech. To really use a different language, you need to *know* the other language.

"Set Proofing Language" can be used to tell Word which language a block of text (or the entire paper) is written in. That tells Word which dictionary to use, and which rules of grammar.

Comments

The next group of icons in the Review tab ribbon is Comments.

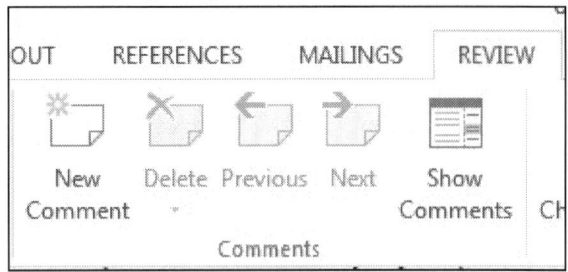

Students don't normally use comments in the papers they turn in, but your instructor may find them a useful way of making "marks" on an electronic version of your paper. (Or if you are editing a draft paper for a collaborative group project, you can tell your co-workers why you made the changes you did.) If you click on New Comment (keyboard shortcut Alt-I, then m), Word will create a box to the right of your paper, in which you may type your comments. After you click back in the main text, a small "balloon" stays in the margin to show that there's a comment hidden therein.

What text gets highlighted? If your cursor is on a word, that word will be highlighted. If the cursor is in a space, it's the word just before the cursor, perhaps the last word in the paragraph. If you highlight some text first, you can have your comment linked to an entire sentence, paragraph, or just one punctuation mark.

The default font for comments, as shown above, is small. If you want your comments to be readable to old folks like your instructor, you'll need to change the style for Balloon Text and Comment Text. See the section on Styles for that.

Your comments aren't always as noticeable as in the image above. Just the small balloons appear in the margin. So if you send a document with comments to someone, you might want to alert them to the fact that you have placed comments in the text. If they click on Show Comments, they'll see them all in the right pane.

By default, Comments are printed in baloons in the the margin when the document is printed. But because the margin that Word uses for comments is wider than your document margins, Word has to shrink the main text in order to provide room on the page for the comments.

The Comments rectangle also provides a way for you to delete specific comments, or to delete all the comments in your document, or to move the the next comment.

Tracking

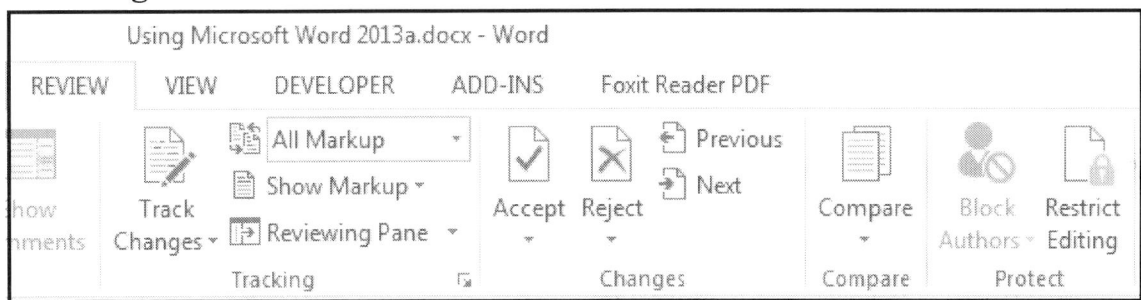

If you turn tracking on by clicking on the top part of the "Track Changes" icon, all your deletions will be shown with dark red ~~strikethrough~~; all your additions will be marked in dark red <u>underlined</u> text. (You can change these colors and options if you want to.) If you are working on a group project and editing a document, tracking can show others exactly what you've changed. (If you want to explain your reasons, you can use the comment feature, as described above.)

All the changes are tagged with hidden codes, showing who made the change. This is especially useful if several people are working on the document in different stages. If you hold your mouse over a change, Word will display for you who did it, and when:

Michael Morrison, 5/16/2013 12:33:00 PM
inserted:
underlined

You can change the name that is displayed by clicking on the small arrow at the bottom right of the Tracking rectangle, and choosing "Change User Name." There are numerous additional options, but we won't cover all those details.

Once you have a marked-up document, how do you get rid of all the marks? You can do it one change at a time by right-clicking on the red changed text, and you'll have the option of accepting the change or rejecting it. You can do it more systematically throughout the whole document by using the "Changes" rectangle.

If you click on the "Accept" icon, Word will accept the edit you are on (if you aren't on an edit, it will go to the next available edit). You can accept changes one by one, or with the small triangle underneath "Accept," you can accept all that are currently visible on your monitor, or accept all changes in the document. The "Reject" menu works in a similar way. If you want to view the changes without making decisions, you can click on the "Previous" and "Next" icons.

"Compare" allows you to compare two documents. This can be useful if someone forgot to turn tracking on, and you'd like to see what changes were made. Or if you have two versions of the document and are not sure which is best, "Compare" will help you identify places in which the documents differ. You select an "original" and a "revised" document (it doesn't matter if you don't really know which one was original), and Word will compare the two documents and display the differences as if changes were tracked. If you "Accept All Changes in Document," you'll end up with the "revised" document.

"Restrict Editing" allows you to restrict the kind of edits that someone else can make. For example, if you send a draft to a member of your group project, you can set it so that the person will not be able to edit the text at all, or force all edits to be in track mode, or allow only comments to be added. Such control is not needed very often.

The View Tab

When word processors were first invented, they displayed the text in Courier font, every letter taking up exactly the same amount of space, just like an old typewriter. That's all the monitors could display. But in a great advancement over typewriters, the printout could be in a proportional-spaced font like Times New Roman. You had to type formatting codes in manually. What you saw on the screen was therefore not what you wanted on the paper, and this sometimes led to problems.

As monitors were improved and graphic displays got better, word processors advanced to WYSIWYG: What You See Is What You Get. Almost every program now displays that way, and the word wysiwyg is falling into disuse, since it goes without saying. Microsoft Word is a wysiwyg program: what you see is what you get when it's printed – so why is there a "view" ribbon, as if you might want to see something else?

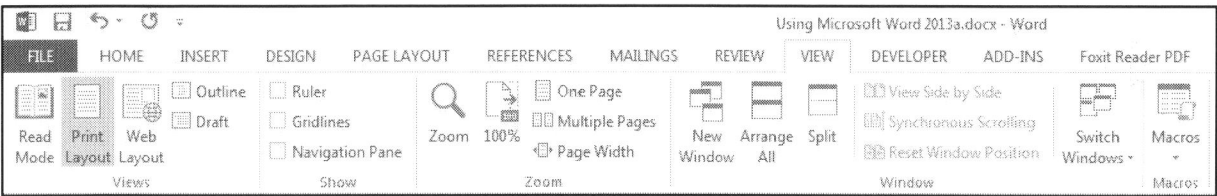

The default setting is "Print layout." That is wysiwyg – what you see on the monitor is the same as the way it will print out – with a minor exception, since you can choose to hide the header and footer (by double-clicking on the crack between the pages, as explained in the Page Layout instructions). It will be hidden on your display, but it will print out.

"Read Mode" eliminates the menu ribbon and makes the text larger. As the name implies, this is for reading – it does not allow edits. What you see is NOT what you get, because the line and page breaks are different.

"Web Layout" also changes the line and page breaks – it shows what the document might look like when saved as a web page, where margins and page widths vary from one computer to another. It is usually difficult to read – there are too many words per line.

"Outline" view is good if you use multi-level outlining, but generally not good for academic papers.

"Draft" maintains the line breaks, but gives a huge right-hand margin. Apparently some people find this useful, but you probably don't need it.

Show/Hide

"Ruler" displays a ruler (in inches, centimeters, or typesetter's picas, whichever you prefer) at the top of your page, and at the left. This can be useful if you are trying to align tables or graphics, but is rarely needed. The units of measurement is set in Options (File tab, then Options, Advanced, Display).

"Gridlines" shows horizontal lines through your text – useful for lining up graphics, but generally not needed for academic papers.

"Navigation Pane," Headings tab, gives you a brief outline of your paper in a pane on the left – outlined by paragraphs in the Heading styles. This can be helpful for a very long paper, if you have used those styles. The "Pages" tab shows miniature pictures of each page in your document. If you click on one of the thumbnail pages, you'll go to the top of that particular page in your document. This can be useful for navigating in long documents.

Zoom

"Zoom" can enlarge all the text without changing the font size. Or it can make it smaller – you have to tell it what you want it to do. The most common settings are given in the icons: 100%, viewing one entire page, two pages side by side, or expanding the page just enough to fill your window. When you click on the Zoom icon, you also have a choice of Text Width – expanding slightly larger than Page Width, cutting the left and right margins out.

An easier way to zoom your document is to use the scroll in the lower right part of the window:

In this illustration, the page is displayed at 130 percent of actual size. If you click on the + icon at the end of the scroll, it will change to 140 percent, and every click after that will increase it another 10 percent. Or you can use your mouse to grab the slider in the middle (hold down the left mouse button) and move it to where you want it.

While we are looking in the lower right corner, we can comment on a few other icons there. To the left of the zoom slider are icons for "view": read mode, print layout, and web layout. The small triangle just above the 130% allows you to slowly scroll down your document.

The easiest way to move around your document is to use the slider on the right. The height of the slider also indicates how much of the document you are currently seeing. In a small document, the slider will be large. In a large document the slider will be small, since you can see only a small portion of the document at any one time.

Window

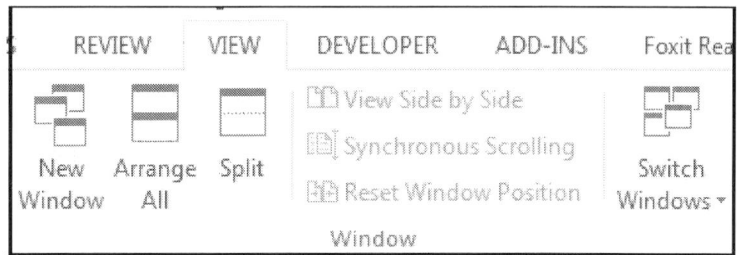

"New Window" opens your document in a new window. That way you can see two parts of your document at the same time. That can be confusing.

"Arrange All" shows all open documents at the same time. (The default is one window above the other; "View Side by Side" will change that.) But unless your monitor is very large, you won't see much of any document. "Split" combines the above two: different parts of your document in different windows. Also confusing. But it is one way to see your bibliography while you are working on the main text.

"Switch Windows" will let you know what other documents are also open, and let you move to one of the others. The icons at the very bottom of your Windows screen will also let you do the same thing. Or use Alt-Tab to rotate between programs.

The last icon in the View ribbon is "Macros." This is a way to repeat frequent tasks – for example, if you often edit text from someone else and have to do a number of search/replace commands, you can put them all into a macro to make it easier next time. Macros are also in the Developer menu, but are too complicated for us to address here.

Developer and Mailings

As the name suggests, the Developer ribbon is for more advanced users. Macros can be created and edited, and all sorts of "under-the-hood" matters can be investigated and changed. We will not attempt to go into those details.

Nor will we say anything about the "Mailings" tab. This can merge a letter with a mailing list, to create personalized letters that aren't really personal. That may be useful for secretaries, but not for academic papers, so we have skipped it.

The References Tab

"References" include several useful features. It may be worth the trouble to learn these features, since they take care of some important details.

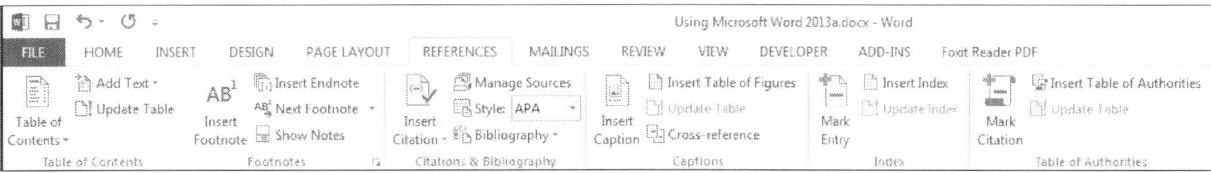

Table of contents

Most academic papers do not need a Table of Contents (TOC), though longer papers and theses do. For this document, we used the TOC feature to automatically create and format the Table of Contents, and to automatically display the correct page numbers. The beauty of the TOC feature is that when we edit any headings or subheads, or the page numbers change, Word will update the TOC as well. The TOC contains links that make it easy for users to click on a page number and jump to the particular section they want.

You probably don't have to use a TOC very often, so we'll just give an overview. When you are working on a thesis or other long paper, you may want to explore some of the options.

First, the TOC feature works only if you are using Styles. This is a good reason to learn to use Styles. The default TOC uses three Styles: Heading 1, Heading 2, and Heading 3. (You can use additional styles if you wish. Click on the Table of Contents icon, then Custom Table of Contents, then Options.) Automatic Table 1 or Automatic Table 2 may be all that you need.

If you would like to exclude certain parts of your paper – you want it to have the Heading 3 Style but not appear in the TOC, for example, you can highlight it, then use "Add Text" to tell Word to *not* show it in the TOC. Or you can add certain parts of your text to the TOC, even though they don't have one of the styles that the TOC normally uses. But normally it's better to use the Styles the way that Word expects.

The format of each level of the TOC is controlled by the Styles menu. You need to edit Style "TOC 1," "TOC 2," etc. The default styles are usually good enough.

After you have made edits to your table, you can click on "Update Table" to have Word recalculate the table. You have the option of recalculating page numbers only, or also recalculating the words in the entry.

Quotes

One of the most important rules in writing academic papers is that you must cite the sources of your information. If you quote something, you must mark it as a quote, and you must cite the source. Otherwise it will look like you are trying to pass off someone else's work as your own. In some cultures this is a compliment to the person you are quoting, but for academic purposes (in America and most other Western nations), it is essential that the instructor be able to distinguish your words from someone else's.

In some cases you should use quote marks if you quote only a single word. That's if it is a highly unusual word, or you are drawing attention to it. In other cases a string of many words may have become part of common English. For example, if you type "out of the frying pan and into the fire" (with quotation marks, so you get that exact phrase) into a search engine, you will find more than a million occurrences. You do not need to use quote marks for such common phrases (however, it may not be a good idea to use such an overused cliché in an academic paper).

If you quote, quote exactly. Don't change any words. If you add anything, it should be inside of square brackets: [   ]. If you leave anything out, you should put in three periods – an ellipsis (…) – to indicate where words are missing. If you start quoting in the middle of a sentence, you may capitalize the word (although some purists put the capital letter inside of square brackets). If the quote contains quote marks, you may change them, so that a quote inside of a quote uses single quote marks. If the quote contains a footnote number or asterisk, you do not need to include it. If there's an obvious typo, you may correct it, although some purists would quote it exactly, and put [*sic*] afterwards to indicate that it's a mistake of the original and not your mistake. If you have changed any italics or boldfacing, you should note that, along with the source, with words such as "emphasis added."

One rule of thumb is to use quote marks whenever you have *five or more words in a row* identical to your source. This does not mean that you can copy an entire paragraph, change every fifth word, and pass it off as your own. You should still acknowledge your source. Many instructors subscribe to a plagiarism-detection service (such as turnitin.com) that will highlight borrowed material.

If you quote more than four or five lines of text, you should put the words into a separate paragraph, and mark it as a quote with indentations instead of quote marks. (The amount of indentation differs according to which stylebook you are following.) This is especially useful if the quote has a quote inside of it; the indentation makes it easier to see where the quote starts and stops. One common format for a block quote is to indent one half inch on both left and right, to single space the paragraph, and to add a blank line before and after it. If your quote comes from the beginning of a paragraph, then indent the first line of your quote.

You must say where you obtained your quote or information. There are several major approaches to citing your sources:

1. Footnotes (*Chicago Manual of Style* and Turabian's *Manual*)
2. Notes in parentheses
   a. Author date, (page) number (Turabian option)
   b. Author number (Modern Language Association)
   c. Author, date, p. number (American Psychological Association)

Find out which style your instructor wants. If the instructor has no preference, choose one *and stick to it.* Do not invent your own style. We'll have more to say about citation style a bit later. We will address footnotes first, since some citation styles use them, and it comes first in Word's menu ribbon.

Footnotes and endnotes

To insert a footnote, position your cursor where you would like the number to be (such as just after the period at the end of your sentence), and in the References ribbon, click on "Insert Footnote." (Or Alt-s, f.) Word will automatically supply a superscripted number, and whisk you to the bottom of the page, where you can type your note. This can be either the source of your quote or some comment you want to add to your paper without disrupting the main flow of what you were saying.

Making footnotes in a word-processing program is *far* easier than on a typewriter! Word will automatically reserve enough space on the page for the text, and will automatically re-number the notes if you move them around. However, if you move the note number itself from one sentence to another, Word will insert a space in front of the number; that should be removed.

The default for footnote text seems to be flush left, no indentation, and 3 points of space added after the paragraph. The font used is based on whatever your "Normal" style is set to, and it is a little smaller. The format can be changed by modifying the "Footnote Text" Style. Here is an example:

¹ This is a footnote, with the separation line above it.
² This is the second footnote.

If you go to the bottom of the page, and right-click on the footnote number, you will see some Note Options. You can also get this by clicking on the tiny arrow in the lower right part of the Footnotes rectangle:

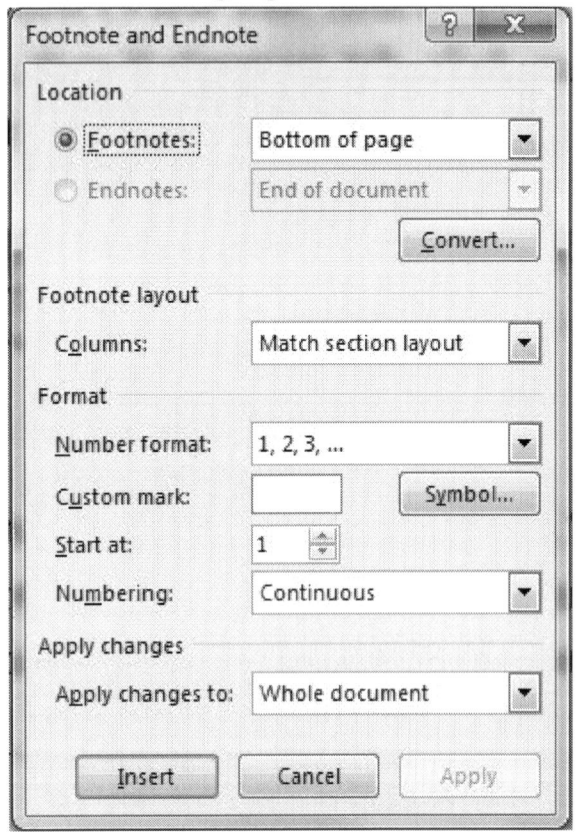

- o Location – the default is usually correct: bottom of the page.
- o Convert: You can change all footnotes to endnotes, or vice-versa. Footnotes are generally preferred because the reader doesn't have to flip pages.
- o Number format. You can use letters of the alphabet, Roman numerals, or symbols. The default is usually correct: Arabic numerals.
- o You can start at a number other than one, if you need to.

o Numbering: You can start renumbering in a new section – in most cases that means a new chapter.

Word automatically inserts a line between the main text and the footnotes at the bottom of the page. This is called a footnote separator. To change its appearance, go to the View tab ribbon, click on Draft view, then go to the References tab, and click on Show Notes. They appear in a small window at the bottom of the page. Click on the triangle to the right of "All Footnotes," and you'll see a drop-down menu, as shown below.

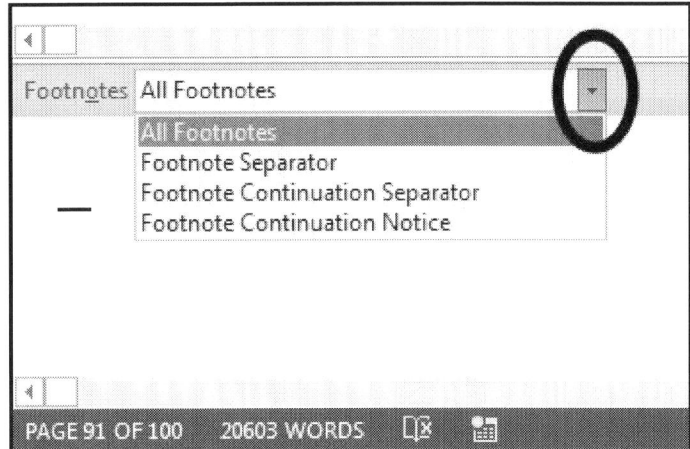

Choose Footnote Separator, and you can remove the indentation, or replace the line with something else. (A Footnote Continuation Separator is the line that's used when a footnote has to continue from one page to another. The default is that it is the entire width of the page, unlike the regular separator. This supposedly alerts readers that what they see at the bottom of one page started on the previous page, but few readers notice the difference.)

Citations & Bibliography

When you quote something, or if you just want to credit the source of something you have paraphrased, how do you do it? Let's look at the Reference Ribbon, the Citations rectangle:

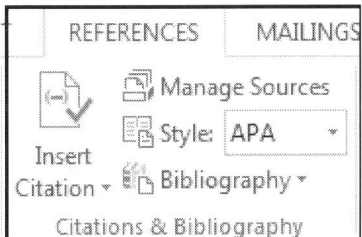

If you mouse over the icon on the left, Word will explain what it's for: "Credit a source of information by citing the book, article, or other material it comes from. You can choose from a list of saved sources, or add a new one. Word will format citations according to your selected style."

The first thing you should do is to select which style to use. In the image above, APA has been selected. You may also choose Chicago, Turabian, MLA, Harvard or other styles. This should be done first because different styles ask for different bibliographic data.

Your next step is to click on "Insert Citation," and then "Add New Source." Word will then give you a form telling you what bibliographic data needs to be entered. You may not like having to get all this bibliographic data, but you need it for the Works Cited section of your paper anyway, and you might as well have Word take care of the commas, periods, and other details. And if you ever use this book again, you won't have to get all the data again. Here's what it asks for APA style, with sample data typed in:

If you click on "Show All Bibliography Fields," you will see options for a number of other bits of information that might be relevant. In the example above, we might have noted that this is the eighth edition, and it has several editors in addition to the author. If you click OK, Word will then insert a citation for you according to APA style: (Turabian, 2013). If we click in the words themselves, we'll see the words shaded, as text that Word has generated:

1. (Turabian, 2013).

Now, while the citation is highlighted, if we choose a different style, Word will adapt it. If we choose MLA, Word will display (Turabian). If we choose Chicago style, Word will display (Turabian 2013). Word takes care of the commas, dates and other details, so your citations can be consistent.

In most citation styles, you will need to add the page number; Word cannot do this for you! You can do this manually, or you can edit the citation and let Word take care of the punctuation details. After you click inside of the citation, a small triangle appears in the lower right to indicate that you can see a menu for further options:

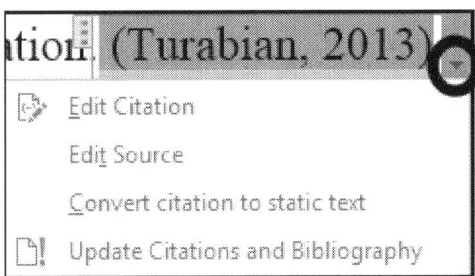

If you click on the triangle, you can edit the citation (to add a page number), edit the source information (to change the book's details), or convert the reference to ordinary text.

You need to include page numbers for all quotes unless you are quoting electronic documents that don't have pages (the location numbers in Kindle, for example, can change depending on the size of the font you want it to display). If you add page numbers by using Edit Citation, then Word will add a comma, or not, whatever is correct for the style you have chosen to use. If you later decide to switch to a different style, Word will fix the comma so that it's right for the new style. So it's good to let Word take care of the commas.

So far we have done one citation. What if we want to quote from the same book at a later time? Now it gets easier: If we click on the Insert Citation icon, we will see a menu of sources to choose from. This includes the data we have already put into the database. So far, we've put in only one book, so it's at the top:

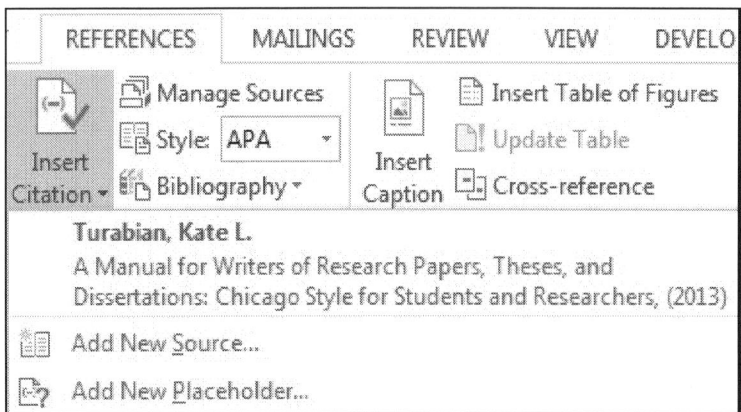

If we simply click on the Turabian entry, Word will put a new citation where our cursor is: (Turabian, 1996). No need to worry about re-typing or spelling it correctly. We'll still have to edit it with a page number.

What if we don't have all the bibliographic data with us while we are typing? Then we can "Add New Placeholder," and get back to it later.

"Manage Sources" lets us edit the information we have put in, *either in this document or in others.* That means that the work we do for our current document will be useable in other future papers, possibly in future courses. In the new paper, go to "Manage Sources," click on the source you need, and click on "Copy" to make it accessible in the current document.

If you would like the bibliographic data for a book, then go to www.worldcat.org/advancedsearch – this database contains more than 10 million titles from more than 10,000 libraries around the world. If it's been printed, they probably have it. Even better, they will give you the bibliographic data in the format that you want. Find the book in their site, then look for "Cite/export" in the upper right. You can choose from APA, Chicago, Harvard, MLA, or Turabian. Then you can copy and paste the info from your browser to Word's "New Source" data box. Save yourself some keystrokes and spelling errors.

In "Style," you can change to several other citation styles, if you don't like the way one appears. In most cases the information transfers over seamlessly, although it cannot supply data you didn't type in. For example, if you were originally in APA style and put only initials for the author's first names (which is OK for APA style), and Chicago style wants them spelled out, it can't do that for you. But if you initially told Word the full name, then Word will remember it for you.

The last and best timesaver comes when you need to do your Works Cited section. Go to the end of your paper and click on "Bibliography." The three built-in formats are not correct. So click on the option at the end: Insert Bibliography. If you click on that, presto, it's all done, already alphabetized:

> Aaseng, Rolf E. *A Beginner's Guide to Studying the Bible* . Minneapolis: Augsburg, 1991.
>
> Turabian, Kate L. *A Manual for Writers of Research Papers, Theses, and Dissertations: Chicago Style for Students and Researchers.* Chicago: The University of Chicago Press, 2013.

This one happens to be Turabian style, with the year at the end. If you want a different style, just choose a different one and Word will re-format it for you. You may want to make minor edits, such as putting in a page break before your "Works Cited" subhead. If you want more space between the entries, or other changes, you can modify the Bibliography style in the Styles menu. (Very few papers have a complete bibliography of all relevant research, and instructors usually want to see only those books that you actually used, so "Works Cited" is the best description of what you want.)

Bibliographic data can be tedious, but Word makes it far easier for you.

Captions

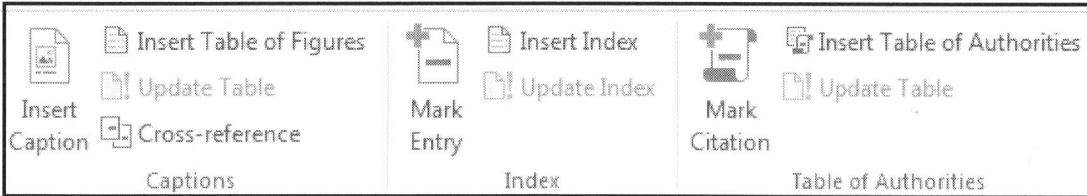

Word can place captions with images, tables, and other objects. The default is small italics – it is helpful to be a little different than the body text, so the reader realizes it is a caption rather than a continuation of the main text. If you want a different default font, change the Caption style. Unfortunately, the text is not anchored to the image or object, so if they move, the caption may be in the wrong place.

Captions and labels are always labelled and numbered. This enables Word to create a "Table of Figures" with links to the pages that each image is on. If you want a table of figures, this can help. If you want captions that are anchored to the image, one way to achieve that is to create a table for them – one column, two rows. The image can be in the top cell, the caption in the bottom. Then they stay together. Tables are as difficult to position as images are, and can jump around if you make edits in earlier pages, so you should position these objects after you have the main text nearly finished.

Index

If you want an index at the end of your document (not needed except for really long documents), Word provides a somewhat-automated way to achieve it. You can highlight terms or phrases you'd like to index, and click on "Mark Entry." Word automatically shows codes at that point, so you can see the entries you make. It also keeps the "Mark Entry" box open, assuming that you are likely to want to mark additional text. After you go through your document marking text, then at the end you click "Insert Index." Word will insert everything you have marked, in alphabetical order, along with page numbers for each item.

"Table of Authorities" is designed for legal documents, to compile a list of cases and laws that have been cited in the paper.

The File Menu

Last, we come to the first tab: File. The keyboard shortcut is Alt-f. Unlike other tabs, it does not display a ribbon – the menu choices are in a vertical bar on the left. Perhaps other Word menus will adopt this look in future editions, but for now it may involve some extra clicks.

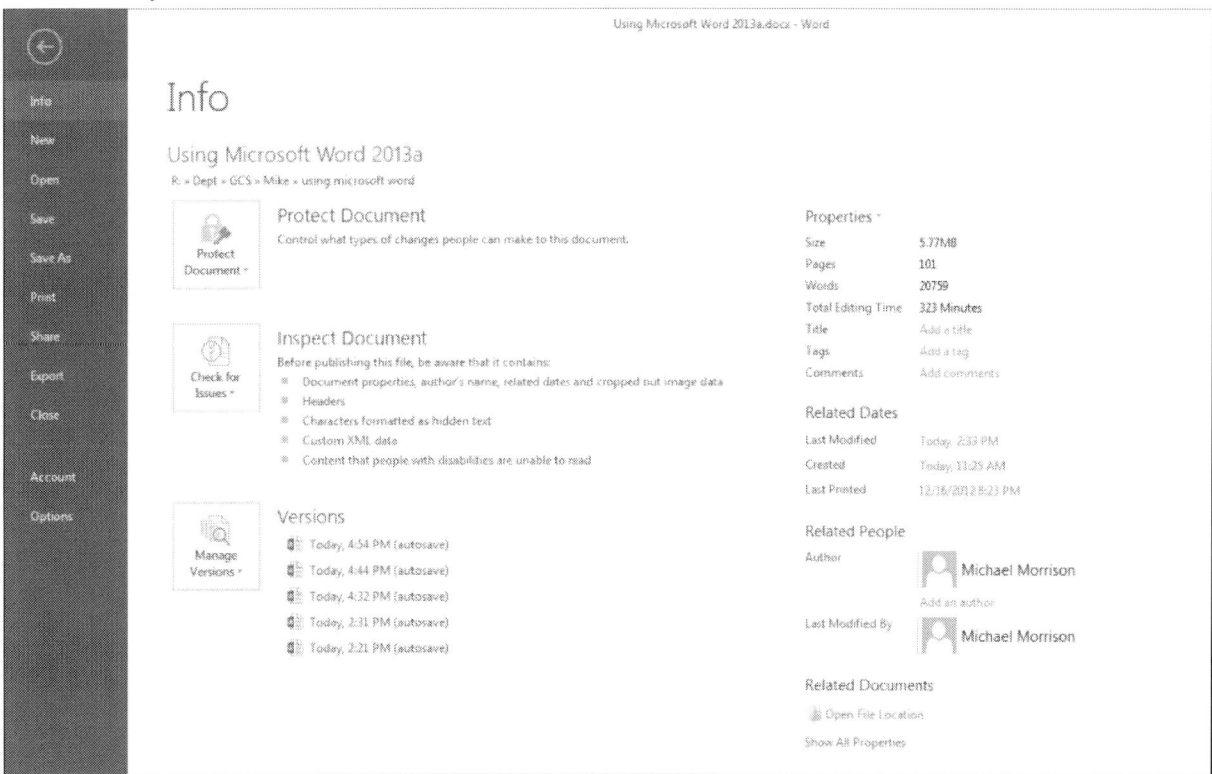

This is one way to save your document, and I hope you have already done that several times by now. But we will point out a few features you might find helpful.

1. The page opens with "Info" about your document and special features it may contain. It shows recent auto-saved versions, in case you want to revert to one of them. It even shows how long you have been editing the document.

2. "New" opens a menu of possible page formats. For academic papers, pick the blank one.

3. "Open" enables you to navigate in your computer to open an existing document. There are a few features here that might be helpful.

    a. On the right side are listed documents you have opened recently. Click on any of them to open it.

b. You can also choose to open from SkyDrive, or on your computer, or you can "add a place."

    a. You have to have a Microsoft account to use SkyDrive – your files are stored "in the cloud," in a Microsoft computer. You must be connected to the Internet to use this.

    b. Your computer is the traditional way to save files. The good part of storing files on your computer is that your files are accessible even if you're not connected to the Internet. The bad part (in the eyes of some people) is that the files are not accessible from other locations.

        Unfortunately, your computer is not as accessible as before – you have to do more navigating. Word will display the folder of your current document, and some of your recently used folders, but if you want something else, you have to "browse," starting at your current folder. Once you click on browse, you'll see a navigation window. There are several features here that are helpful.

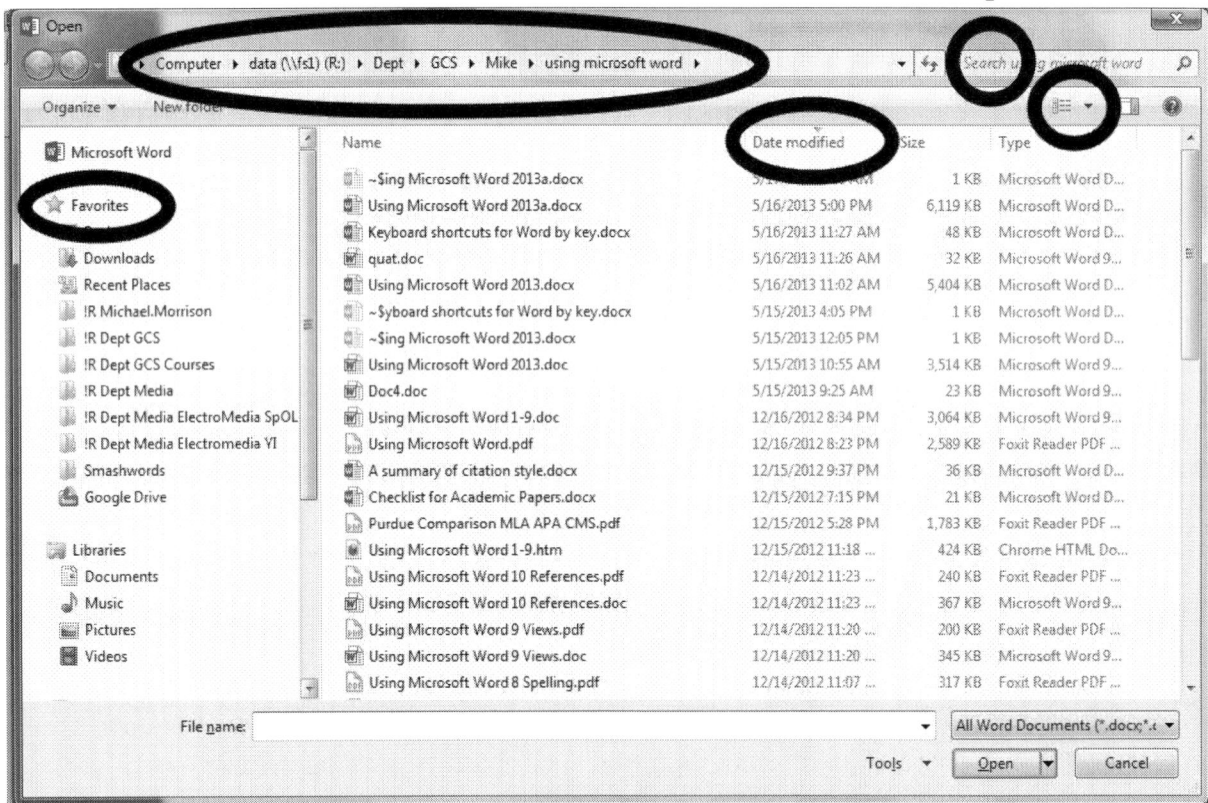

    1. At the top of the window is displayed the path of the folder you are currently in. The words in the path are

links, and this is an easy way to navigate backwards in your folders. You can click on the word "Computer," for example, to move there. Or you can click on one of the small triangles to move to a subfolder in one of the folders. You can double-click on a subfolder to move to it, or you can right-click and choose "New," then "Folder" to make a new one.

2. The good part about browsing is that you can now use the "search" box in the upper right corner of the Open dialog box. If you have forgotten where a document is, this can be helpful – it will search the folder you are currently in and all the subfolders in it. Search for a unique word that's in the document.

3. The "Views" icon can change the display from icons to a simple list, to details. In the details view (shown above), one column is labeled Date Modified. Click on it to sort all the documents in that folder by date – in that way it is easy to identify the one that you've worked on most recently. Click on "Name" to sort them alphabetically.

4. You now have access to your "favorites" folder, in which you can include your commonly used folders.

5. The entire window is re-sizeable. You can use your mouse in the lower right corner to drag the window larger or smaller.

c. In "Add a Place," you can add other cloud services.

4. Now let's go back to the file menu. "Save" is a very important feature, since programs sometimes freeze and lose data. Word automatically makes a backup copy every 10 minutes, but you could still lose a lot of data if you forgot to save your document. The keyboard shortcut for Save is Ctrl-s; there is also a small icon on the Quick Access Toolbar in the upper left of your screen – it looks like a floppy disk just to the right of the Word Logo. (Floppy disks are rare nowadays, but we don't have a better icon.)

    If it's a new document, "Save" will give you you the "Save As" dialogue box, asking which folder should be used, and what to name the document.

    Word will automatically supply the extension ".docx," so you don't need to. The default folder is probably "Documents" or "My documents" (that can be changed in Word Options). To move to a folder that is backwards in the folder structure, click on words in the pathway. If you want to save to a flash drive in a USB port, for example, you'd need to navigate first to your computer, and then to the letter assigned to that flash drive.

5. "Save As" (Alt-f, a) is useful if you wish to save the document with a new name or location, while keeping the old name. This is one way to preserve a history of your document. Each day (or each hour, depending on your anxiety), you can save the document with a different name. If you don't like the May 12 version, you can go back to your computer and pick up an earlier one.

    Save As gives you a display similar to Open, with options to save to SkyDrive, your computer, or some other place. It shows the current folder (perhaps the most likely place to save a new edition), or other recent folders, or you can browse. With any of these options, you get a traditional folder explore menu box, as show above in "Save." If you want, you can skip the Save As menu and several clicks by using the shortcut F12 right from your document.

    One surprising thing is that if you make this box shorter, you will actually get *more* options for saving your document:

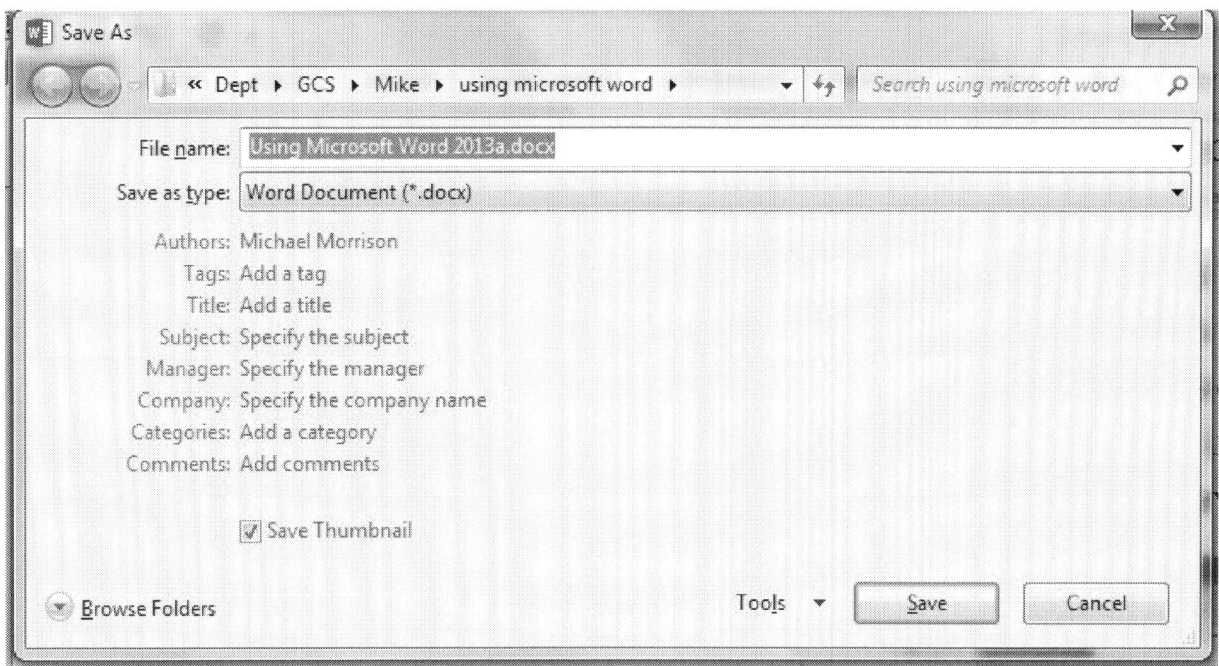

You can change who the author of the document is, you can add tags (indexing codes), a title, subject, company name, or other comments. These all reside in the hidden "properties" of the document.

If you click in the "Save as type" box, you have a choice of what "type" of document you wish to save this as. One commonly used option is to save it as a PDF document, or as html document for posting on the internet.

6. "Print" (Alt-f, p, or simply Ctrl-p) will launch you into a redesigned print menu, where you can choose how many copies to make, which printer to use, which pages to print, some of the printer settings, etc. Word automatically displays a preview of the page you are on, including its images (as shown below); you can scroll to see other pages previewed.

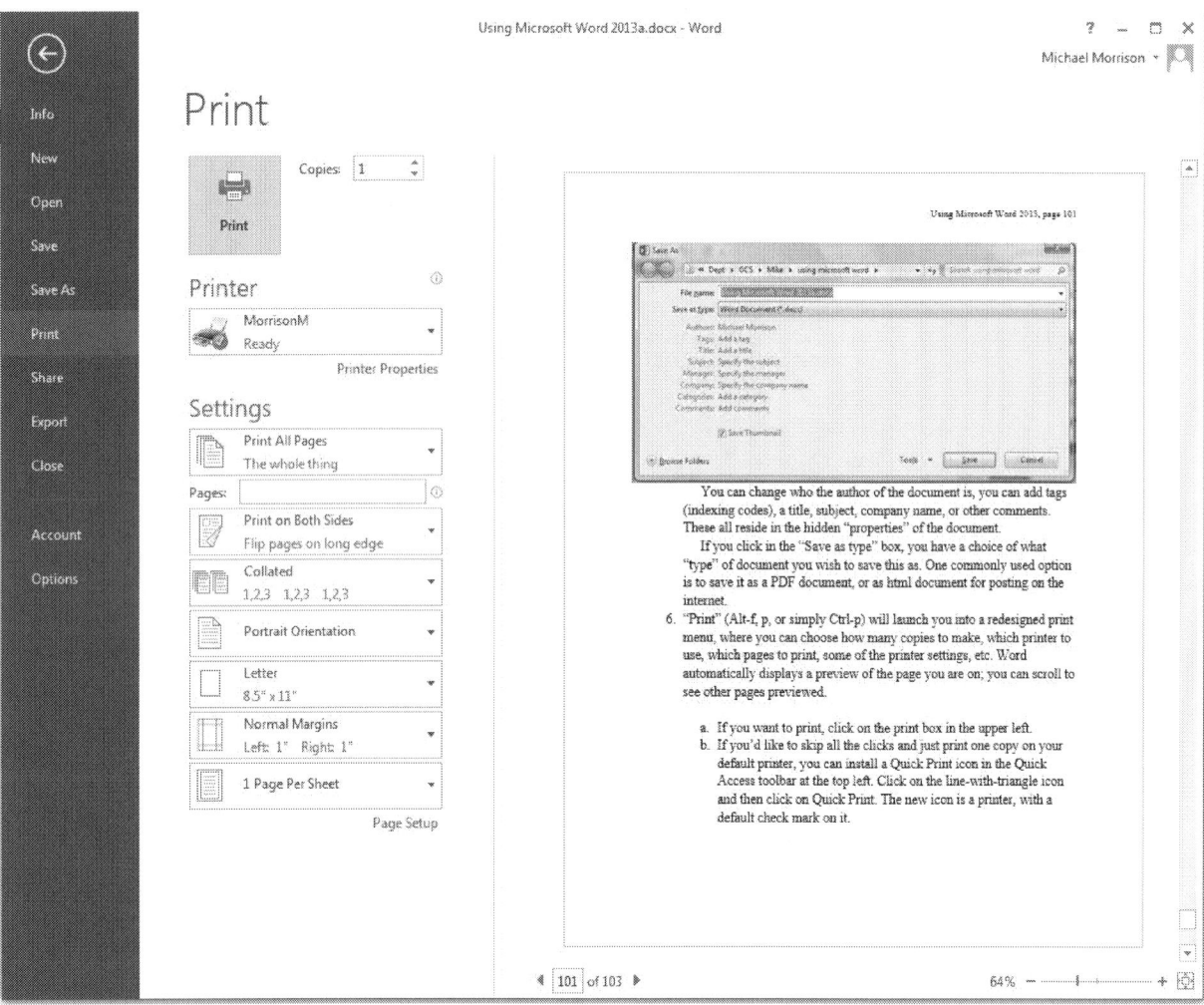

a. If you want to print, click on the print box in the upper left.

b. If you'd like to skip all the clicks and just print one copy on your default printer, you can install a Quick Print icon in the Quick Access toolbar at the top left. Click on the line-with-triangle icon and then click on Quick Print. The new icon is a printer, with a default check mark on it.

7. On the File menu: "Share" gives you options for sending your document to Skydrive and simultaneously giving someone access to it, or sending it to Outlook to email to someone, or sharing in other ways.

8. "Export" can save the document as a PDF, or other file types. Save As can do the same things.

9. "Close" exits this particular document but Word remains running. If you have not saved your changes, Word will ask if you want to.

10. "Options" is a portal into some of the inner workings of Word.

If you want to exit the program entirely, click on the small x in the upper right corner.

Checklist for Academic Papers

___ Paper size: 8.5 x 11

___ Margins: 1 inch

___ Font size 12 for all body text (footnotes and headers can be 10 or 11)

___ In ordinary text, first line of each paragraph is indented

___ No extra space between paragraphs

___ Short quotes are marked with quote marks

___ Quotes longer than four lines are marked with indentations

___ Citation given for all quotes

___ For encyclopedia articles, authors and name of articles are given

___ All citations include page number, if from a print edition

___ Works Cited starts on new page

___ Works Cited is alphabetized by authors' last names

___ Book and journal titles are italicized

___ Dates are given for each source

___ For electronic sources, also give the date of the print edition it is based on

___ URL given for all internet sources

___ Student's last name is in header of document

___ If requested, student's last name is in beginning of document name (this makes it easier for the instructor to find your paper in a list of files – this can be important if papers are submitted electronically).

12613917R00059

Printed in Great Britain
by Amazon.co.uk, Ltd.,
Marston Gate.